MONSTERS
AND DEMONS

MONSTERS AND DEMONS

CHARLOTTE MONTAGUE

CHARTWELL
BOOKS, INC.

CONTENTS

Introduction ... 6

INTRODUCTION

Throughout the history of human civilization, stories of monsters and demons abound in every culture. From Biblical beginnings, to medieval folklore, and right up to the present day, there have always been tales of unusual characters living alongside humans. In the mythologies of these monsters and demons we learn that each culture has its dreaded beasts, and we discover the very human fear of 'the unknown' that goes back to the beginning of time. It could be argued that there is a universal soft spot for monsters, demons, supernatural ghouls and even ancient mythological baddies. From being terrified of ghastly beings lurking under our bed when we were children, to growing up and being nostalgic for those childish beliefs, monsters represent the last bit of mystery and wonder in the world, and it is from this curiosity that fascination in the subject continues to grow.

· ·
BIBLICAL BADDIES

Monsters and demons feature largely in religious texts. The Leviathan is a demonic sea serpent from the Hebrew Bible. In this story, the Leviathan resembles a dragon, with plumes of smoke pouring from its nostrils and fire blazing out of its mouth when it roars. It is so huge and powerful that when it moves it has the effect of stirring up the ocean, and causing the ground to tremble. There is one thing that strikes fear into the beast, however, and that is a tiny

Blue devils consign sinners to all-consuming hellfire. A wall painting in Ukra Kidane Mekret Christian monastery, Tana Lake, Bahir Dar, Northern Ethiopia. Tana Lake is the source of the Blue Nile river in Africa.

worm named Kilbit. Leviathan lives in fear of the minute creature clogging up its gills, and stopping it from breathing. In medieval Christian demonology, Leviathan became one of the seven princes of hell, presiding over the sin of envy. He is seen as a hugely powerful force of evil, linked to Satan, and capable of killing God's creatures by drowning them in the sea. In some versions of the legend, his mouth is described as the 'mouth of hell', a portal into which sinners are thrown on the day of judgement, never to return to earth.

MYTHICAL MENACES

Ancient Greek mythology features a myriad of hybrid creatures and demonic witch-like characters. The Gorgons, a trio of winged demons, are a famous example. Medusa and her two hideous sisters, Stheno and Euryale, have nests of hissing snakes in the place of hair, freaky staring eyes, lolling tongues, flared nostrils, and tusks like those of pigs. Their faces are so incomprehensibly ugly that if human eyes ever fell upon them, the tragic spectator would turn immediately to stone. In the ancient legend, the warrior Perseus is ordered to kill Medusa, and is armed with a sword, an invisibility cloak and a mirrored shield, so he is able to approach her undetected and destroy her without their eyes meeting. His task is successful, taking her hissing head off with one clean slice to the neck with his sword, but as she died, two mutant sons, Pegasus and Chrysaor, sprang from the bloody wound. Cerberus, another figure of ancient Greek mythology, is a three-headed being; each head being able to see the past, present and future respectively. The heads, like Medusa, hiss with snakes, and further snakes cover its body. The job of the Cerberus is to guard the gates of the Underworld, and prevent any doomed souls

from escaping back out to the land of the living and also prevented the living from entering Hell.

FOLKISH FREAKS

Folklore refers to a collection of local legends and fables which belong to certain communities. These stories often date back hundreds of years and feature numerous tales of diminutive creatures which lurk in the woods, as well as demonic spirits which inhabit houses and terrorize its residents. In Norse mythology, we find a character which has become a popular source of inspiration for fiction writers. The concept of the troll differs according to certain regions. In some areas, it is thought of as a small and ugly goblin-like character, with a manipulative and mischievous nature. In other areas, it is a stupid, violent brute, with a single, bulging eye in the middle of its forehead, much like in the ancient Greek myth of the Cyclops. The current perception of the troll as a fearsome but dimwitted giant, however, was born from the popularization of the 1841 Norwegian fairy tale *Billy Goat's Gruff*. In modern times, this image is perpetuated through works of fiction such as the hugely successful *Harry Potter* franchise.

THE UNDEAD

In contemporary fiction, characters from beyond the grave are as popular as ever. Vampires and zombies have been given 21st-century makeovers, and are now seen as attractive and romantic figures, doomed to languish in the prison of eternal life. In the original myths, and in the versions that exist in various cultures, revenants (the undead) are depicted entirely differently. In China, the closest monster to the Western vampire is known as a Jiang Shi. This spirit sleeps in a coffin during the day, and emerges at night, moving stiffly due to rigor mortis. It hops on one leg and its constantly-decomposing arms are permanently outstretched in front of itself. It hunts for humans, and when it has selected its victim it plunges in its sharp fangs, and sucks out the life force in order to ensure its own survival. It is usually believed that a person who dies and returns from beyond the grave must have lead a truly awful life of crime. In some cultures a person who is afflicted with becoming a revenant may have been murdered, committed suicide, or not have been buried in the correct fashion. In the case of becoming a Jiang Shi, there is a strange belief that if a pregnant cat jumps over a coffin, the corpse inside will transform into a vampire.

ELUSIVE CRYPTIDS

Today, a general belief in the existence of monsters and demons is wearing thin. However, there is such a thing as a 'cryptid'. This type of monster is believed to exist by some parties, but not taken seriously in scientific communities. The most infamous examples of cryptids are Bigfoot, the Loch Ness monster and the Yeti. These characters have had people puzzled for generations. People who hunt for these cryptids have discovered all sorts of 'proof', however these are often revealed to be hoaxes. Numerous photos of Bigfoot have been taken, but on closer inspection it is often decided that the subject of the picture is simply a tall man in a hairy suit. Alleged Yeti footprints are always

Illustration from a 16th century French bestiary of a mythical amphibious creature, about to devour a sheep.

revealed as manmade tracks, and as for the Loch Ness monster, there is simply no concrete evidence for its existence. Loch Ness frequently plays host to teams of scientific researchers with state of the art equipment. Despite the occasional interesting reading recorded during these investigations, no incontrovertible proof has ever been found. Yet people still believe. Further to these world-famous beasts, are tales of many other creepy cryptids. In the region of Point Pleasant, West Virginia, was once a local beast which terrorized the community for a whole year in the 1960s. This character appeared at night and usually on Highway 62. It was dark grey in colour, enormously tall and wide, and with glowing read eyes situated at its shoulders. It had huge wings, and would fly alongside cars, emitting a high-pitched screech. In addition to this, the random appearance of a strangely-behaved man in the town coupled with many residents reporting electrical disturbances to their phones and televisions encouraged rumours that there was an extra-terrestrial dimension to the events unfolding in Point Pleasant. After a year, reports of encounters declined, but the flying cryptid, known as the 'Mothman', was never forgotten.

BIG SCREEN BEASTS

It is on the big screen that monsters, gruesome critters and mythological demons really come to life. When you think of monster movies, the 'classics' spring to mind first. Between 1923-1960 Universal Studios released a series of movies which came to be known as 'Universal Monsters', and instantly became cult classics of the B-movie genre, these included: *The Phantom of the Opera, Dracula, The Wolf Man* and *Frankenstein*. These quintessential monster movies have stood the test of time and inspired many affectionate remakes. Today, the portrayal of monsters has come a long way since the days of Lon Chaney Jr and Bela Lugosi. Cinema-goers are now used to incredible special effects, with CGI and other technologies perfected to such a degree that seeing really is believing. However, back in the golden age of cinema, other techniques of depicting monsters were used. Unfortunate actors would spend hours upon hours having make-up applied and prosthetics attached to them. In the 1954 movie *Creature from the Black Lagoon*, the actor playing the creature, Ben Chapman, had to wear his sea-monster bodysuit for up to 14 hours a day. This would overheat easily in the Californian sun, and so Chapman spent any time he was not required on set, cooling off in the lake on the back-lot, occasionally asking to be hosed down.

The many monsters, demons, spirits, ghouls and critters that fill myths, legends and folklore of the world continue to fascinate us. We grow up learning about biblical fables, fairy tales and urban legends, each story fuelling our imagination. In addition to this, the world of movies undoubtedly plays a huge part in keeping this interest alive. While sophisticated modern audiences would not be terrified by Ray Harryhausen's skeletal warriors in the 1963 movie *Jason and the Argonauts*, today they may cower behind their popcorn at the 3D Medusa in 2010's *Clash of the Titans* remake. However, this does not necessarily make the old movies outmoded; CGI and 3D technologies have breathed new life into the old classics, but they cannot recapture the charm of the originals. From the monster movies of the early 20th century, to the blockbusters of today, the appeal of beastly characters remains; the fascination preserved for the next generation.

Section One:
DEVILISH DEMONS

DEMONS ARE EVIL SPIRITS, usually associated with the Devil, and believed to exist in hell. They can travel between the underworld and Earth, and can be commanded to perform all manner of dreadful and destructive deeds. It is in biblical texts that tales of demons persist, and it seems they belong to many religions. The Leviathan, of the Hebrew Bible, is a terrifying demonic sea serpent that can shake the very core of the Earth with the slightest movement. Lilith, is a different kind of demon. She is a character from Hebrew mythology, and is known as a storm demon. As well as being a bringer of disease and death, she is also a Succubus, an evil temptress who seduces men and drains them of their energy in order to replenish her own.

SATAN

Satan is the ultimate demon. As the principal opponent of God, faith and morality in the Christian, Islamic and Jewish religions, he strikes fear into the hearts of all believers. He is the greatest and most powerful force of evil known to man, and at his command his legions of lesser demons will incite hatred and bring about destruction, chaos and death.

THE ULITIMATE DEMON

Satan is not just a figure in major world religions, he also appears in pagan and other alternative faiths, as well as featuring in many non-religious, folkloric cults. At different times, and in varying cultures, he has gone by many names: the Devil, the Prince of Darkness, Lucifer, Beelzebub, Belial, Mephistopheles, Samael, Satanael, Mastema, Iblis, and Shaitan, to name but a few. Yet, as the destructive force of evil, he always has one aim: to tempt humanity into wicked ways, thereby bringing about the destruction of moral order, progress, rationality, and civilization in general.

MESSENGER OF GOD

In early Hebrew texts, we find the words 'Ha-Satan' or 'the Satan' used to describe a divine being who is sent by God to test the faith of human beings and report back on the results. The term 'Ha-Satan' is translated variously as 'opponent', 'prosecutor', 'adversary' and 'accuser'. At this point, Ha-Satan is clearly a servant or messenger of God, entirely under His control. Ha-Satan's job appears to be dreaming up ways of testing God's faithful followers, as seen in the Book of Job. Ha-Satan points out to God that Job is only morally good because he has everything a man could want. For this reason, God grants Ha-Satan permission to test Job by taking everything away from Job and allowing him to suffer, thereby finding out if he will remain faithful during his tribulations.

SATAN'S TRANSFORMATION

Over time, Satan's role as God's helper, responsible for testing an individual's moral fibre in times of trouble, changed quite radically. We see the beginnings of this transformation in the esoteric writings of the Hebrew Apocrypha, texts written by religious thinkers and holy men that are not considered part of the sacred scriptures of the Bible. In the Book of Enoch, we find that Ha-Satan became Satanael, the leader of a group of angels known as the Grigori, or Watchers, a race of angels who have fallen from heaven. These angels married human women, giving rise to a race of beings known as the Nephilim. In this incarnation, Ha-Satan resembles Mastema, an evil angel from Hebrew folklore, whose name means 'hatred' or 'persecution'. Mastema flatters God in order to gain power, controlling a host of demons and obtaining permission to visit disaster and destruction on humanity, through hideous means such as sending plagues and pestilences.

Satan attended by demons in human and animal form.

THE DEVIL REBELS

In the Book of Enoch, Satanael is sometimes referred to as Satariel, connecting him to the good archangels Michael, Gabriel, Raphael and Uriel, who were his brothers before his fall from heaven. In these apocryphal texts, Satan is not always seen as wholly evil; his role is to tempt human beings but, as a servant of God, he hopes that they will find the strength to resist. This interpretation is also found in other religious Hebrew writings, such as the Talmud and the Kabbalah, where some sympathy is expressed for the unpopular role of the 'obstructor'.

In Christian readings of the Bible, Satan takes on a much more central role. Instead of being God's servant, sent to test humanity, he becomes God's opponent, a force for evil that is extremely powerful. This transformation occurs most obviously in medieval times, where Satan becomes 'the Devil'. The word 'Devil' can be traced back to the Greek 'Diabolos', or 'slanderer'. The Devil is an entity that is not under God's control; he seeks to lead people away from God, for his own destructive ends. The Devil speaks to the darkest forces within human nature, and is able to persuade individuals to rebel against God, to sin, and to lead lives that are entirely evil, against God's teachings.

....

SERPENTS AND PLAGUES

As well as God's chief opponent, the Devil also commands all demons and evil forces in the world. He takes many different forms. He is sometimes a serpent, as in the story of Genesis, where the serpent tells Eve to eat the forbidden fruit, causing humanity to be cast out of the Garden of Eden and condemned to a life of toil and suffering. He may also be a dragon, as in the Book of Revelation, or a 'prince of the air', causing pestilence and plague. He may also take complete posses-

sion of individuals, in which case his victims will cause all manner of evil, until he is driven out of them through exorcism.

....

WAR IN HEAVEN

Satan, or the Devil, is also connected to — and sometimes confused with — other fallen angels, such as Beelzebub, Belial, and Lucifer. In Hebrew and Christian writings, Belial appears as a wicked, worthless demon in the guise of two angels sitting in a chariot of fire. He leads humanity into idolatry, the worship of false gods. Lucifer, the light bearer, is the name given to the Devil before his fall from heaven. In early Christian theology, Lucifer was one of the brightest angels in heaven, but he wanted to be as powerful as God, so he rebelled and started a war in heaven. He was cast out of heaven by God, along with his followers, and seeks to wreak his revenge by leading humanity into wickedness.

There is some controversy among religious scholars as to whether the Devil and Lucifer are one and the same. However, in popular interpretations of the Bible, the Devil is seen as intelligent, resourceful, ambitious and full of pride, just as Lucifer was. It is sometimes assumed that the Devil, or Satan, is the fallen angel Lucifer in his earthly, corrupt form.

SHAITAN AND IBLIS

Satan, or the Devil, plays an equally important part in the Islamic faith, as Shaitan. Shaitan, in the Arabic language, denotes distance, so the name comes to mean a being that leads humanity away from Allah, or God. In the Qur'an, this being is called Iblis, a jinn or genie. Jinn are supernatural beings who appear both in Arab folklore and religious teachings; they have a parallel existence to humanity, and like humanity, are blessed (or cursed) with free will, so that

they can act in good or evil ways. However, unlike human beings they have no real bodies, but are made of 'smokeless flame'.

Iblis is an evil jinn or genie who is full of pride, and has the power to cast bad thoughts into the minds of human beings. Interestingly, Iblis has no other real power – as in the Christian religion, he relies on the weakness of individuals to bring misery and destruction on the world. This idea that the Devil's evil power comes about through playing on human failings, such as pride, envy, anger and lust is very prominent both in the Christian and the Islamic traditions.

· · · ·
REFUSAL TO BOW

The Qur'an tells the story of how Allah commanded his angels to bow down before the first man, Adam. Iblis, who like the other angels had free will, but who was full of self-love and pride, refused to do so. Iblis thought he was superior to Adam, since Adam was made of clay, while he himself was made of smokeless fire. For this sin, of disobeying God, and of ranking himself higher than another being of God's creation, Iblis was dubbed 'Shaitan', meaning enemy, rebel, or evil one. God cast him out to roam the earth, where he has the power to tempt humanity away from the path of righteousness. In the Qur'an it was Iblis who tempted Eve in the Garden of Eden, causing the rupture between God and man. As a punishment, Iblis will be cast into hellfire on judgement day. Iblis knows this will be his fate, and is intent on gaining as many followers as he can before his eventual demise.

· · · · · · · · · · · · · · · · · · ·
DANTE'S DEVIL

In Dante's *Divine Comedy*, written in the 14th century, Satan appears as a three-headed monster, carrying various sinners in his mouth, ready to rip them apart. One of these

includes Judas Iscariot, Christ's betrayer. Satan resides in the ninth circle of hell, trapped in a frozen lake, beating his six huge wings.

Milton's *Paradise Lost* portrays Satan in a more sympathetic light, showing him as ruthless and selfish, but also ambitious, proud and independent; chafing under the immutable rule of God. In Christopher Marlowe's 17th-century play, *The Tragical History of Doctor Faustus*, we meet the Devil as Mephistopheles, a winged demon who features in German folklore. Doctor Faustus is a scholar who calls on Mephistopheles and sells him his soul, in exchange for pleasure. Mephistopheles appears again in Johann Wolfgang Goethe's late 18th-century play, *Faust*, and in Thomas Mann's 1947 novel, *Doctor Faustus*.

The Faust legend continues to be a relevant one today, pointing up a perennial human dilemma – how much will we sacrifice our principles to fulfil our ambitions? In the various interpretations of the legend, we are reminded that the Devil does not force us to sin, but that we ourselves, of our own free will, knowingly allow corruption and excess into our lives.

· · · · · · · · · · · · · · · · · · ·
DEVIL WORSHIP

Contrary to popular belief, the worship of Satan has never been a common practice. Much of what we would call witchcraft was developed, not by pagan religions, but by Christian priests in the medieval period, who seemed to have an unhealthy preoccupation, not to say a fanatical obsession, with the occult in all its forms. The well-known image of Satan as half-man and half-goat, with horns, trident, and a forked tail developed in this period. This concept does not come from the Bible, but from various other sources, one possible influence being the classical Greek gods such as Pan and Dionysus, and from imagined pagan deities such as Baphomet. Baphomet was a pagan god mentioned in the trial transcripts of the 14th-century Knights Templar, where individuals were accused of heresy and burned at the stake. He was later revived in the 19th century by occult writer Eliphas Levi, who portrayed him as a 'Sabbatic goat', sporting horns, wings, and women's breasts.

....

WITCH-HUNT

In reality, there were many non-Christian religious practices flourishing in Europe in which various deities were honoured, but between the 14th and 18th centuries, the Christian Church chose to represent these pagan rituals as devil worship. This led to persecution of witches on a huge scale, especially in northern Europe. Some historians believe that, during this process, pagan deities such as the horned god associated with nature, hunting, and sexuality, were demonized thus becoming 'the Devil'.

Since the late 19th century, neopagan and New Age belief systems have emphasized the positive qualities of Lucifer, rather than Satan, as the bringer of light to the human race, and this can be seen in alternative faiths. The founder of the Theosophical Society, Helena Blavatsky, named her journal Lucifer. Similarly, the Wicca movement has tried to reclaim the ancient pagan 'horned god' associated by Christians with the Devil, as a force for good. According to many New Age doctrines, Satan must be recognized as part of our own negative or destructive tendencies. This view is not so very far removed with certain biblical stories about the role of Satan, as well as having connections with literary interpretations by such writers as Milton and Goethe.

....

CHURCH OF SATAN

Another view of Satan, often emphasized by those who call themselves Satanists, is that humanity must come to accept its carnal, rebellious and independent spirit. In doing so, we must focus on earthly matters, reject the idea of the existence of God, and celebrate the here and now. According to this view, propounded by groups such as the Church of Satan, founded by Anton LaVey in the 1960s, Christianity and other world religions have operated as a repressive force throughout history, which must be challenged if we are to achieve our full potential. Other Satanist groups, known as theistic Satanists, share the Judaeo-Christian belief system, but focus on magic and ritual, worshipping Satan as a deity. In the 1980s, Satanism became the focus of a huge moral panic concerning ritual child abuse on a grand scale; however, as it transpired, there was little evidence to suggest this was a widespread practice, and the panic eventually subsided.

XV The Devil. A 19th century French tarot card.

BEELZEBUB

Beelzebub is one of the principal demons of antiquity. His origins are obscure, but he appears in the Old Testament, and later in Christian demonology, in various guises. In some accounts, he is the same person as Satan, in others, he is a mere servant of the 'Prince of Darkness'. However, in whatever form he appears, he is regarded with fear and loathing, since he causes human beings to behave in the most bestial of ways. He is behind all manner of sinful activity, from gluttony and pride to demonic possession. In the New Testament, he is even said to take possession of Jesus, giving Him the ability to drive out demons.

LORD OF THE FLIES

The name Beelzebub means 'Lord of Zebub'. 'Zebub' may be the name of an actual place, perhaps a great city or lofty citadel ruled over by the Lord. However, it is also the word for 'flies' in the Hebrew language. It is unclear which of these meanings the word 'zebub' has, but we know that 'Ba'al Zebub' was the name of a god worshipped in the Philistine city of Ekron, since this is mentioned in the biblical Book of Kings. Scholars have speculated that describing this god as 'Lord of the Flies' may have been a way for Semitic people to show their hatred of the Philistines, by calling their god a 'god of the dung heap', where flies gather.

Whatever the early origins of the demon Beelzebub, it is clear that he later became a powerful figure in the Jewish, and later the Christian, world view. The Book of Kings, in the Old Testament, tells a story that King Ahaziah of Israel had an accident, in which he injured himself. The king sent a messenger to Ba'al Zebub to find out if he would recover, since Ba'al Zebub was thought to have the gift of seeing the future. The prophet Elijah then condemned the king, because he should have asked Yahweh, the god of the Jews, for advice, rather than the Philistine god.

PRINCE OF DEMONS

In some esoteric biblical texts, such as the Testament of Solomon, which forms part of the Apocrypha, Beelzebub appears as the prince of demons, the highest-ranking demon of them all. He is often associated with the morning or evening star, called Hesperus or Venus. The Testament of Solomon tells the story of how Beelzebub was once an angel, but fell from heaven, along with numerous other angels, including Abezithibou, a one-winged angel who later became an adversary of Moses, and who waits in the Red Sea to be released by the wind demon, Ephippas. Beelzebub also cites his great adversary as the Almighty God, Emmanuel, who can dispel him with a powerful oath. In this version, Beelzebub is seen as one and the same person as Satan (who, confusingly, later became known as Lucifer), since he is the principal opponent of the Hebrew God.

We also learn something of Beelzebub's nature in the Testament of Solomon. When Solomon asks the demon about his special powers, Beelzebub replies: 'I bring destruction by means of tyrants; I cause the demons to be worshipped alongside men; and I arouse desire in holy men and select priests. I bring about jealousies and murders in a country, and I instigate wars.' This notion of Beelzebub as the demon of anger and jealousy later changes, in the medieval period, where he is assigned a place as one of the seven princes of hell, the force behind the deadly sin of gluttony.

····

OCCULT PRACTICES

Beelzebub also tells Solomon about occult practices that will help the king find out about the spiritual world. He says: 'Listen, King, if

you burn oil of myrrh and frankincense along with saffron... and light seven lamps during an earthquake... and if, being ritually clean, you light them at the crack of dawn, just before the sun comes up, you will see the heavenly dragons and the way they wriggle along and pull the chariot of the sun.'

In the Gospel of Nicodemus, a fifth-century religious text, Beelzebub is cited as 'the prince of perdition and chief of destruction.' He is accused of being behind the crucifixion of Jesus, and of plotting to bring Jesus down to hell after His death, instead of letting him ascend to heaven. In the gospel, the name Beelzebub becomes Beelzebul or Beezebub, and is often used as a secondary name for Satan, who is cursed as the enemy of the Lord.

····

DEMONIC POSSESSION

In the gospels of the New Testament, Beelzebub continues his reign as the prince of demons. Mark, Matthew, and Luke all mention an episode where Jesus is accused by the Pharisees of driving out demons by the power of Beelzebub. The Pharisees believed that Jesus was possessed by Beelzebub, which gave him this demonic power.

········

DEVIL'S MAGIK

Beelzebub as 'Lord of the Flies' took on an ever more threatening dimension in the writings of medieval occultists. In the 16th century, Johann Weyer, a physician and follower of the German magician Agrippa, wrote an influential book called *On the Illusions of the Demons and on Spells and Poisons*, published in 1563. In it, he advised against the persecution of witches, adopting a sceptical attitude influenced by his scientific and medical studies, and questioning the claims of witchcraft. He argued that magic was impossible, and that those purporting to be witches were suffering from mental confu-

Woodcut of a monster for Edward Fenton's *Certain Secret Wonders of Nature* (1569).

sion. However, he seems to have believed in demons, although some believe that his descriptions of them may have been ironic.

••••

KING OF THE HEAP

Whatever his personal beliefs, Weyer made an extensive list of some of the major demons in Christian texts that went on to influence many other religious thinkers. He described Beelzebub as originally belonging to the angelic rank of cherubim, and told how he led a successful revolt against his leader, Satan. Weyer claimed Beelzebub to be the chief servant of Lucifer, emperor of hell, and said that he presided over the Order of the Fly, marshalling all kinds of poisonous and unclean winged insects to his side. This role as the Lord of the Flies harks back to the Old Testament, and the early Semitic religious texts, in which Beelzebub appears as the ruler of the dung heap. According to Weyer, Beelzebub is second-in-command to the Devil, Satan, or Lucifer, as he was variously known in medieval times.

••••

SEXUAL ENCHANTMENT

The preoccupation with demons, and in particular with Beelzebub, continued throughout the medieval period. Sebastien Michaelis, a Dominican monk, took up the theme in his writings, building on the work of Weyer and others. Unlike Weyer, Michaelis was not a very humane or rational man and he was involved in many witch trials. He persecuted the women remorselessly, often condemning them to be burned at the stake. He wrote a number of books, including one called *Histoire Admirable de la Possession d'une Penitente*, published in 1612. In it, he described the demonic possession of a young nun called Madeleine Demandols de la Palud, who had accused a priest, Father Louis Gaufridy, of sexually enchanting her.

According to Madeleine, Father Gaufridy's breath had become an aphrodisiac to her, through the power of the Devil, and in this way he had forced her to dabble in witchcraft. She told how, as a witch, her body was invaded by Beelzebub, and other demons, and claimed that these would only leave her when Gaufridy died.

••••

DEVIL'S MARKS

According to Michaelis, Beelzebub spoke to him through Madeleine, telling him that over 6,000 devils had possessed her and other nuns who were also being tried for witchcraft. Gaufridy was duly arrested and found to have 'devil's marks' upon his body. He was tortured until he confessed, and then burned at the stake in Aix-en-Provence.

The most memorable aspect of the book was the extensive list of demons that Michaelis attached to it. He placed Beelzebub in the first hierarchy of demons (descended from the angel orders: seraphim, cherubim, and thrones), just below Lucifer, and beside Leviathan. He claims that Beelzebub, Lucifer, and Leviathan were the first three demons to fall, and that Beelzebub's particular role is to tempt humanity with the sin of pride. Michaelis sees each demon as being opposed by a saint. Beelzebub's opponent, according to him, is St Francis of Assisi.

••••

THE SEVEN DEADLY SINS

Demonology was a major interest among religious thinkers in the medieval period, who loved to categorize the wicked behaviour of the demons in gory detail. Each demon was seen as having specific characteristics, was responsible for a particular kind of sin, and was at its most energetic at a certain time of year (Beelzebub being very active in July, apparently). The medieval demonologist, Peter Binsfeld, wrote *The Confessions of*

Warlocks and Witches in 1589, pairing each of the seven deadly sins with a demon: gluttony with Beelzebub, lust with Asmodeus, greed with Mammon, sloth with Belphegor, wrath with Satan, envy with Leviathan, and pride with Lucifer.

DEMON FASCINATION

In the centuries that followed, the continuing fascination with demons found its place in literature. John Milton's *Paradise Lost*, published in 1667, describes Beelzebub as the right-hand man of Satan, having fallen from heaven with others angels of the rank of cherubim. Milton depicts Beelzebub as intelligent and ambitious, but using his considerable talents for corrupt ends. Like humanity itself, Beelzebub the fallen angel turns away from God and seeks to amass power for his own ends, embodying the sins of pride and lust. Milton's work was unique at the time in making parallels between the sinful behaviour of the fallen angels, such as Beelzebub, and human beings, so that the demons were seen as part of human nature, rather than entirely separate, evil entities controlling it.

LORD OF LUST

John Bunyan's *Pilgrim's Progress*, which first appeared in 1678, characterizes Beelzebub as the lord of lust, who sets up Vanity Fair, a marketplace in the city where he attempts to entice the honest pilgrims Christian and Faithful with worldly goods and honours. Beelzebub also appears at the Wicket Gate, shooting travellers with arrows to stop them from going forward on the path to God. Once again, as in medieval times, Beelzebub is associated with the baser side of human nature, in particular with a desire for worldly pleasure and success.

PRINCE OF IDOLATRY

In the Salem Witchcraft Trials of 1692, Beelzebub was repeatedly cited as corrupting witches, a subject discussed by the fanatical Puritan minister Cotton Mather in his pamphlet *Of Beelzebub and His Plot*. He was blamed for corrupting the witches, and for causing them to behave in ungodly ways, as well as giving them special evil powers, such as invisibility. This theme reappeared in 1801, in Francis Barrett's *The Magus*, a compilation of occult texts. Here, Beelzebub was seen as the prince of idolatry, a false god worshipped by those who practised the dark arts.

A powerful image of Beelzebub as a huge, ugly fly came from Collin de Plancy's *Dictionnaire Infernal*, published in 1863. This was an illustrated A-Z of demons, both famous and obscure, from Abigor to Zaebos. As if under the influence of the demons himself, de Plancy started out as a non-believer, under the influence of the great sceptic Voltaire; however, he then became a fervent religious follower, altering his descriptions of the demons to fit his new-found Catholic faith.

BEELZEBUB TODAY

Today, Beelzebub continues to excite the imagination, appearing as a character in several computer games, including Playstation's *Castlevania: Symphony of the Night*. Here, he appears as a living corpse with insects feeding on it, which has the ability to breed more flies and send them out to attack the hero. In modern times he has been continually referenced in literature, film, and music, most memorably in William Golding's *Lord of the Flies* and Stephen King's *Salem's Lot*, as well as in the lyrics to 'Bohemian Rhapsody' by the rock group Queen.

LEVIATHAN

The Leviathan is a huge sea serpent described in detail in the Hebrew bible. He is a kind of dragon; he breathes fire, smoke pours from his nostrils, and his mouth is lined with jagged teeth. Scales resembling shields protrude along his back, so that javelins, spears and arrows simply break when they hit his body. He is a fearless creature and so terrifying that even the bravest of warriors cower at his slightest movement.

THE LEGEND

According to ancient accounts, Leviathan is so big that 'the depths churn like a boiling cauldron' when he thrashes about, and the sea is stirred up 'like a pot of ointment'. It is said that only Yahweh, the Jewish God, is more powerful than he. Yahweh can break the head of the Leviathan into pieces, cut up his flesh, and give it to his people in the wilderness to eat. Despite his enormity, he is frightened of a tiny worm called Kilbit, who could clog his gills and stop him breathing. It is foretold that at the end of time, Yahweh will kill the Leviathan, thus bringing to a close his reign of terror.

. . . .

BEHEMOTH AND LEVIATHAN

The myth of Leviathan continues in later Jewish culture, where he shares control of the elements with Ziz, the demon of the air, and Behemoth, the demon of the land. In the Book of Enoch, a mystical Jewish text, Leviathan is described as a female monster living in the depths of the sea, whose partner is Behemoth, the lord of the wilderness on land. When God created these male and female demons, Behemoth and Leviathan, he went on to kill the female, so that the two could not mate and their offspring could not take over the earth and therefore bring

destruction to the human race. Legend has it that on the day of judgement, God will kill all the demons and serve out their flesh, including that of Ziz, another enormous creature whose wingspan is so great he can block out the sun.

In medieval Christian demonology, Leviathan became one of the seven princes of hell, presiding over the sin of envy. He is seen as a hugely powerful force of evil, linked to Satan, eating God's creatures or drowning them in the sea. In some versions of the legend, his mouth is described as the 'mouth of hell', into which sinners are thrown on the day of judgement, never to return. Thomas Aquinas, the great 13th-century religious thinker, describes Leviathan as the first demon to punish sinners when they enter hell. In Milton's *Paradise Lost*, Leviathan becomes an ambiguous symbol of the power of evil. Later, the term 'Leviathan' was used to mean any large sea creature, such as the whale in Herman Melville's 1851 novel *Moby Dick*.

. . . .

THE 'GOOD' LEVIATHAN

The philosopher Thomas Hobbes, writing in the 17th century, uses the legend of Leviathan in a more benign way, as a political metaphor for the all-encompassing power of the state. The body of the Leviathan, in his view, is the people, who look towards the sovereign, to rule them through consent. In this way, Hobbes conceived of the 'body politic' as a combination of democracy and autocratic rule.

Various new interpretations of the biblical legend have been put forward in recent times. Some believe Leviathan and Behemoth were early names given to dinosaurs. Others, such as New Age thinkers and the Satanist, Anton LaVey, have associated Leviathan positively, with water, life and creation.

. . . .

SEA SATANS

Ancient tales of such sea monsters abound in many cultures. In Norse mythology, we find the Jörmungandr, a serpent that is so long he encircles the earth and is able to grasp his own tail. For this reason, Jörmun-gandr is known as the World Serpent. His opponent is the thunder god Thor, and it is believed that when Jörmungandr is defeated and lets go of his tail, the world will end.

Throughout the history of human civilization, we find serpent demons in myths and legends who symbolize the terrors of the deep, in a time when sailors had little knowledge of what they would encounter when they set out to sea. In early Syrian myths we encounter the seven-headed sea monster, Lotan. He lives in a palace at the bottom of the sea, and is responsible for storms, floods, and icy weather. He is sometimes seen as the pet of Yam, the God of the Sea; in other instances, he is thought of as a sea god himself. Lotan's main adversary is Baal Hadad, a Semitic storm god, who wears the headdress of a bull, and carries a thunderbolt.

MAMMON

Mammon, the false, evil god of greed, is worshipped by those who value only money and material wealth. The Christian ethic, developed over many centuries, teaches that Mammon is an entirely negative symbol of avarice; and in the 21st century, as more and more lives are caught up in the machine of global capitalism, it seems that he continues to be as powerful and seductive a deity as he was in ancient times.

THE TWO SIDES OF MAMMON

Since earliest times, philosophers, politicians and religious thinkers from all cultures have warned us about the dangers of excessive materialism in undermining moral values and breaking apart social bonds such as fam-ily and community. Yet there is also a more positive aspect to the myth, in terms of its connection to the ancient Greek god Plutus, who symbolized wealth as good fortune, peace and plenty.

GOD OR MAMMON?

The word 'mammon' comes from several sources, including the Aramaic, Syrian, Greek and Latin words for 'riches' and 'money'. We find many references to Mammon in the Bible, from the Old Testament, where he is a symbol of greed and avarice, to the New, where he is personified as a false idol.

Jesus' Sermon on the Mount, one of the founding texts of Christianity, is reported in the gospel of St Matthew, and contains a criticism of the worship of Mammon: 'No man can serve two masters; for he will either hate the one and love the other; or else he will hold to the one and despise the other. Ye cannot serve two masters, ye must either serve God or Mammon.' In the sermon, Christ was specifically criticizing the idea, prevalent in the established church at the time, and continuing until today, that extreme wealth is compatible with a moral Christian life devoted to seeking spiritual fulfilment.

····

THE SIN OF GREED

In the Middle Ages, Mammon was often associated with Satan and Beelzebub. He was named as one of the seven princes of hell, not surprisingly, personifying the sin of greed. In some cases, 'mammon' was used as a term for wealth, while in others, he was seen as a deity. In the 12th century, bishop Peter Lombard noted, 'Riches are called by the name of a devil, namely Mammon, for Mammon is the name of a devil, by which name riches are called according to the Syrian tongue.'

In the 13th century, the religious thinker Thomas Aquinas described the sin of avarice as 'Mammon being carried up from Hell by a wolf, coming to inflame the human heart with Greed'. The 14th-century Franciscan monk and biblical scholar Nicholas of Lyra also named Mammon as a demon, in a passage commenting on the Gospel of St Luke.

MAMMON IN LITERATURE

In literature, Mammon is often represented as being similar to other ancient gods, including the Golden Calf (the false god who was worshipped by the Israelites, invoking God's wrath) and the Greek God Plutus. Plutus was the god of wealth, and is also connected to (and sometimes confused with) the ruler of the Underworld, Pluto, who personifies the dark forces of avarice, lust, and greed. According to ancient Greek mythology, Plutus' mother was Demeter, the goddess of the harvest, and was brought up in a time of plenty, symbolized by the cornucopia, or horn of plenty. Plutus was also seen as symbolic of peace and good fortune in civilizations, cities and communities.

However, writers in medieval times tended to ignore this benign account of wealth giving rise to peace and plenty, and instead emphasized the more demonic aspects of the myth. In Canto VII of Dante's *Divine Comedy*, Plutus appears as a wolf, guarding the fourth circle of hell, which houses the sinners who have spent their lives as hoarders and wasters. Today, Plutus features in the video game *Dante's Inferno*, based on the 14th-century classic, where he is a wolf able to solidify gold with the beam of his eye.

····

THE FAERIE QUEEN

Mammon was often alluded to in English literature, memorably in Edmund Spenser's epic poem, *The Faerie Queene*, where the god guards a cave full of treasure. In Milton's *Paradise Lost*, Mammon appears as a fallen angel, who has sinned by valuing earthly goods over heavenly virtue. He is also a popular figure in works of occult writers such as Collin de Plancy, whose luridly illustrated *Dictionnaire Infernal* shows Mammon as an anxious, throned figure, seated on a treasure chest and hugging bags of money.

Hell, a detail from the painting *The Last Judgement* by medieval artist Fra Angelico (1395–1455). Demons drive the damned into Hell, where the wicked are tormented. At the very bottom Satan chews on three of the damned, and grasps two others.

OBSERVATIONS

As well *Historical* as *Theological*, upon the NATURE, the NUMBER, and the OPERATIONS of the

DEVILS.

Accompany'd with,

I. Some Accounts of the Grievous Molestations, by DÆMONS and WITCHCRAFTS, which have lately annoy'd the Countrey; and the Trials of some eminent *Malefactors* Executed upon occasion thereof: with several Remarkable *Curiosities* therein occurring.

II. Some Counsils, Directing a due Improvement of the terrible things, lately done, by the Unusual & Amazing Range of EVIL SPIRITS, in Our Neighbourhood: & the methods to prevent the *Wrongs* which those *Evil Angels* may intend against all sorts of people among us; especially in Accusations of the Innocent.

III. Some Conjectures upon the great EVENTS, likely to befall, the WORLD in General, and NEW-ENGLAND in Particular; as also upon the Advances of the TIME, when we shall see BETTER DAYES.

IV A short Narrative of a late Outrage committed by a knot of WITCHES in *Swedeland*, very much Resembling, and so far Explaining, *That* under which our parts of *America* have laboured!

V. THE DEVIL DISCOVERED: In a Brief Discourse upon those TEMPTATIONS, which are the more Ordinary *Devices* of the Wicked One.

By **Cotton Mather.**

Harris for *Sam. Phillips.* 1693.

Title page of Cotton Mather's book
Wonders of the Invisible World 1693.

ASMODEUS

In Christian demonology, Asmodeus is listed as one of the seven princes of hell. Asmodeus presides over sexual desire, and causes this to become deviant, perverted, and transgressive. Of the seven deadly sins, Asmodeus is the demon of lust, and is also associated with lechery, lasciviousness and revenge.

HYBRID DEMON

Asmodeus has been represented in many different guises throughout history, often featuring serpents, cockerels, dragons, lions and bulls. In Collin de Plancy's *Dictionnaire Infernal*, the demon is depicted as a hideous being composed of different animal parts, including four heads, bat wings, clawed feet and a spiny tail. The name Asmodeus comes from the ancient Zoroastrian religion, which was written in a language called Avestan. In Avestan, 'aesma' means 'wrath', while 'daeva' is the word for 'demon'. In the Jewish mystical text the Kabbalah, Asmodeus is said to be the bastard son of a female demon, or succubus, named Agrat Bat Mahlat, and the great King David.

....

BANKER OF HELL

Asmodeus makes an appearance in the biblical scripture the Book of Tobit, where he falls in love with a woman named Sarah. The unfortunate Sarah tries to marry seven times, but each time Asmodeus kills her husband on the couple's wedding night. The only suitor of Sarah's to survive is Tobit, a young man who is protected by the biblical archangel Raphael. On Raphael's advice, Tobit cooks a fish's heart and liver on a bed of cinders, so that it gives off a stench and clouds of smoke. This wards off Asmodeus, who runs away to Egypt. Later, the demon is trapped by the archangel and bound so that he cannot cause any more mischief.

Asmodeus is a wicked demon who causes all kinds of evil, but his main feature is his carnal lust. In the Jewish Talmud, the story is told of how he married Lilith, the storm demon, and how the pair of them reigned together, in a union of destruction and death. He is also mentioned in the Testament of Solomon, which forms an esoteric part of the Old Testament known as the Apocrypha. In this episode, King Solomon asks Asmodeus about his nature, and finds out that the demon hates water and the creatures of the sea, as well as the birds of the air, because these remind him of the beauty and goodness of God.

....

THE PRINCE OF LECHERY

Many Christian theologians of the medieval period were obsessed by demons, so Asmodeus, the demon of lust, was the subject of intense curiosity. Asmodeus was said to be very powerful in the month of November, and to have 72 legions of demons under his control. He was also reputed to be one of several kings of hell, working for Lucifer, the emperor of hell. As well as inciting humans to sexual lust, he also presided over the gambling houses in hell, and was responsible for the madness and greed that caused people to gamble until they lost all their belongings. Johann Weyer, a Dutch demonologist writing in the 16th century, claimed that in hell, Asmodeus is the chief banker of the baccarat table.

. . . .

THE LEGACY OF THE DEMON

Not surprisingly, Asmodeus was a popular figure among the demons of literature, and was described as 'the prince of lechery' in the German legend of Friar Rush, which was printed in many cheap editions in the 17th century. The legend tells of how the demon takes human form as Friar Rush, a pimp and a prankster, who finds pretty women for the monks of his order to enjoy at night. At long last, after many adventures, his true identity is discovered, and he is expelled from the mon-astery. In this tale, the demon's ingenuity and sense of humour is emphasized, an idea that continues in novels and short stories up until the 19th century, where he is often depicted as handsome and good-natured, though walking with a limp. The reasons for his limp vary according to different myths; in some, he is said to have fallen from the sky while fighting with the Devil, while in others he limps because he walks with the gait of a cock, one leg raised to show his claws.

Today, Asmodeus survives in many popular role-playing games such as *Dungeons and Dragons*, *Pathfinder* and *Hellgate*. Many features of the original concept of Asmodeus have been retained, such as the different animal parts, while others, such as tentacles, have been added.

BELPHEGOR

The demon Belphegor, often depicted as a grotesque, devil-like man with claws and horns, is sometimes known as 'the disputer'. His purpose is to lead mankind to evil by using the promise of wealth as a tool of seduction. According to the Kabbalah, he can guide men to making ingenious inventions or important discoveries, and when these men are fully seduced by financial rewards, they will have turned to the dark side.

. . . .

BAAL-PEOR

The demon Belphegor is thought to have derived, in earliest times, from a god named Baal-Peor. Baal-Peor was the deity of a mountain in the Moabite plain, where according to the Old Testament, the tribe of the Israelites visited during their wanderings. Legend has it that this god was very licentious, and that it was worshipped by both men and women of the Moabite tribe in the form of a great phallus. In some biblical stories, Baal-Peor was mentioned as taking the form of a cone or tree branch.

In the 16th century, the legend of Bel-phegor was extended when he became one of the seven princes of hell, ruling over the seven deadly sins. The German bishop and theologian Peter Binsfeld made a classification of demons in 1589, associating Belphegor with the sin of sloth. Binsfeld was a fanatical persecutor of witches and warlocks, who claimed that all information that they gave about demons, even when it was extracted under torture, should be believed. Basing many of his claims on such confessions, he alleged that Belphegor achieved his wicked aims by tempting people to dream up clever plans and tricks, instead of getting down to hard work. It was also claimed that Belphegor was particularly active in the month of April.

As well as inciting individuals to laziness, Belphegor was thought to be responsible for a great deal of licentiousness among weak-natured men and women. In the Old Testament, the god Baal-Peor had been described as sexual in nature, and it was claimed that the Israelites tempted by him, had become involved with Moabite women. The Israelite men had fathered children by the Moabite women, and had also been led into orgies with them. As a result of this ability to lead men astray, when invoked by a human male, Belphegor could appear as a beautiful, enticing young woman.

．．．．
LIVE HUMAN SACRIFICE

Another 16th-century demonologist, the German physician Johann Weyer, made an exhaustive study of demons, entitled *On the Illusions of the Demons and on Spells and Poisons*, which was published in 1563. (Weyer numbered the total demon population at 7,405,926 exactly, adding that they served under 72 princes.) He characterized Belphegor as a permanently open-mouthed demon, arguing that the name Phegor means 'crevice' or 'split'. He speculated that Belphegor may have lived in a cave, where people threw him offerings through a crack in the rock. This idea may have been linked to legends in the Semitic religious culture that Belphegor was worshipped with faeces, dropped into his open mouth from above, as people defecated over him. Other myths referred to Belphegor as being fed live human victims as a form of sacrifice.

The *Dictionnaire Infernal*, written by demonologist Collin de Plancy, was published in 1818. It did not receive wide attention until in 1863, it was published in a new, illustrated edition. It was this edition, with its gruesome illustrations of many of the demons cited, that caught the public imagination. Belphegor was pictured here, not in his incarnation as a sex goddess, but in his less appealing guise as an ugly old man with horns, talons, and a long, pointed tail, like the Devil.

．．．．
BELPHEGOR'S LEGACY

According to legends of antiquity, Belphegor was sent by the Greek god of the Underworld, Pluto, to cause trouble among humans, particularly married couples. Pluto wanted to know if men and women could live together in harmony. Belphegor did his best to incite disagreement among married couples, but in the end had to admit that it was possible for them to find happiness together. Because of this, Belphegor is often portrayed as a misanthrope, one who hates and distrusts humanity. He appears in various classic works of European literature, including Machiavelli's short story *Belfagor*, in Milton's *Paradise Lost*, and in Victor Hugo's *The Toilers of the Sea*.

Today, Belphegor continues to feature in popular culture. He has many incarnations: as the central figure in the 1927 French horror novel by Arthur Bernède, entitled *Belphégor*, as the name of an Austrian heavy metal band, and as a wicked demon in many popular *anime* and *manga* series.

INCUBUS & SUCCUBUS

The Incubus and Succubus are male and female demons of seduction. At night, they hunt for sleeping humans to mate with. When they have chosen their unconscious partner, they invade their dreams and seduce them. According to varying versions of the legend, they can either appear beautiful and appealing, or frightening and repulsive.

....

NOCTURNAL VISITORS

This type of demon has a long and varied history in myths and legends around the world, and has often been used to explain sexual misbehaviour of different kinds. In the past, if an unmarried woman became pregnant, she might attribute her pregnancy to a visitation by the incubus. Alternatively, if a man raped a woman while she was asleep, he might lay the blame on the incubus. In addition, orgasms occurring in women as they slept, as a result of dreaming, were often thought to be the work of the incubus; while nocturnal emissions, or 'wet dreams' were believed to be the work of the succubus. It was also believed that visitations by such demons could seriously damage the victim's health, resulting in disease or even death. This was a particular risk if sex with the incubus occurred frequently.

Various characters in history were believed to be the offspring of the incubus. In Arthurian legend, the great wizard Merlin was said to be a 'cambion', that is, the child of an incubus and a human mother. (A cambion could also be the offspring of a succubus and a human father). In medieval chronicles known as the Prose Brut, Merlin's mother was cited as a mortal woman named Adhan; his magical powers were, of course, thought to derive from his demon father.

LILU THE INCUBUS

The notion of the incubus goes back to ancient times, specifically to the Sumerian civilization, around the period of 2400 BC. According to the epic poem, *Epic of Gilgamesh*, the Sumerian king was reputed to have been sired by an incubus called Lilu, a demon who wandered about the plains seeking to cause pain and harm to human beings. Some scholars who have studied the period believe that the legend of Lilu arose in an effort to explain perplexing forms of mental illness, in particular, where sexual deviancy occurred. Lilu the incubus was said to seduce women in their sleep, causing intense sexual excitation; Lilitu, or Lilith was the female counterpart of the demon, who appeared to men during erotic dreams, causing nocturnal emissions. Other demons in this category include Irdu Lili and Ardat Lili, male and female storm demons who are said to mate with humans, producing ghostly offspring.

....

SHAPE-SHIFTING DEMONS

In the Christian tradition, the nature of incubi and succubi was the subject of a long and heated controversy over many centuries. One of the founding fathers of Western Christianity, St Augustine, writing in the year 426, claimed that 'sylvans and fauns, who are commonly called incubi, have often made wicked assaults upon women'. Eight centuries later, the theologian and philosopher Thomas Aquinas argued that demons could change shape, becoming a male or female, and could 'take the seed' of a human being so that they could reproduce. If a demon came upon a fertile young woman, he would assume the form of an incubus to impregnate her, using her eggs for the purpose; if the same demon came upon a virile young man, he would change into a succubus, using the man's sperm to sire a child. In this way, the children of demons were thought to be made from human eggs and sperms; however, their supernatural powers would be inherited from the demons. Exactly how they took on the magical attributes of the demons, when they were genetically human, was never explained.

....

RIDDING THE DEMON

Casting out demons and warding off the attacks of incubi and succubi was, from the outset, a tricky business. According to the *Malleus Maleficarum*, a 15th-century treatise on witches, there were several ways to get rid of the demons. If the sign of the cross was made over the victim, the demon might flee; if a confession was made, in which the victim recited his or her sins, this might have the same effect; and lastly, ritual exorcism could be attempted. However, it was claimed by the 17th-century writer Ludovico Sinistra that exorcism had no effect on incubi, who were 'not in the least overawed' by reverence for holy rituals.

SATANIC LOVERS

Myths and legends about incubi and succubi occur in many cultures around the world. In Ecuador, stories are told of the 'Tintin', a dwarf who likes long-haired

women and visits them at night, playing the guitar under their bedroom windows to seduce them. In Chile, the 'Trauco', a horribly deformed dwarf, casts an erotic spell on beautiful young women and then seduces them. The 'Boto' of Brazil, which takes the form of a river dolphin in the daytime, is a handsome young man who seduces women by taking them to the riverside. The Boto always wears a hat, to hide the dolphin's breathing hole on the top of his head.

Similar tales abound in Europe, for example in Hungary, where the 'Liderc', a Satanic lover, is said to fly around the countryside at night. In Africa, too, we find demons such as the 'Tokolosh', a Zulu male demon who is short and ugly. As a precaution against him, Zulu women place their beds on bricks, raising them up so that the little Tokolosh cannot climb up to get them. Among Arabic-speaking people, the legend of the 'Garina' tells of a spirit akin to the succubus, who has sex with men during their sleep. The men know they have been visited because they remember the event in their dreams. Garina are invisible, but it is alleged that people with special prophetic powers, or 'second sight', are able to see them. The Garina often visits a household in the form of a pet dog or cat. If a Garina establishes a relationship with a human male, that man cannot marry, otherwise the Garina will harm the man's spouse.

SACRED PROSTITUTION

The idea of the succubus, while intertwined with that of the incubus, also has a separate history. Her name comes from the Latin 'succubare', meaning 'to lie under'. In medieval times, the succubus was seen as a grotesque, ugly, but highly sexualized creature; in modern representations, she appears as a more conventionally attractive, pretty young female.

According to the Kabbalah, Lilith, Adam's first wife, became a succubus when she left him to mate with the archangel Samael. As well as Lilith, Samael also mated with other succubi, including Naamah, Agrat Bat Mahlat, and Eisheth Zenium. These succubi, as well as Lilith herself, were associated with 'sacred prostitution', esoteric religious practices that honoured the union of god and goddess, and sometimes included sexual intercourse between men and women as part of the church rituals.

A GRIM CONCEPTION

In medieval times, it was believed that the succubus collected semen from men while she was seducing them. She then passed the semen on to the incubi, who visited human females and impregnated them. In most stories, the succubi were seen as wholly evil; however, the medieval writer Walter Map reported a story in which Pope Sylvester II had sexual relations with a benign succubus who helped him progress in his career. The succubus was named Meridiana, and before his death, Pope Sylvester confessed his involvement with her, and died as a repentant sinner.

The incubus concept illustrated in *The Nightmare 1800*, Nikolaj Abraham Abildgaard (1743–1809).

LILITH

Lilith, a snake-like character from Hebrew mythology, first appeared in 4000 BC as a storm demon in Mesopotamia. She, and other storm demons like her, are said to bring disease, illness and death. She is also a succubus and appears to men in their dreams to seduce them. It is thought that when she mates with men, she drains away their strength, using this stolen energy to fuel her nightly hunts.

BRINGER OF DOOM

Some believed that Lilith was the servant of other deities, such as the Sumerian goddess of fertility, Inanna; others, that she was a prostitute, a bringer of shame, death and disease. She was usually portrayed as young and beautiful, but unable to bear children because she could not make milk in her breasts. Lilitu, as she is sometimes called, is often depicted as having talons and wings, like a bird. She would leave her lair at night, whenever a sandstorm blew up, to prey on men and generally wreak havoc in the lives of human beings.

FEMALE PARADOX

This feature of Lilith's nature, her inability or unwillingness to have children, aligned with her youth, beauty and sensuality, points to a continuing paradox that has fascinated men and women alike throughout history. Lilith appears to embody a profound fear of what might happen if women were released from their role as mothers, nurturers, and helpmeets to the male. In particular, in her demonized form, and through her association with the night, she represents a vision of powerful female sexuality that has terrified men since earliest times, and over the centuries, has caused many religious thinkers to teach that women are essentially evil, seducing men with their feminine wiles, but really seeking to harm them.

SEXUAL PREDATORS

Lilith is also connected to demons known as 'lilitu', bird-like creatures with talons and wings, who were sexually predatory towards men. The male wind demon Pazuzu, king of the wind demons, was said to have control over the lilitu. Like Lilith, lilitu are described as being the handmaidens of Inanna, the sacred goddess of love, fertility and warfare in the Sumerian pantheon. Inanna was particularly associated with sensual love, rather than marriage, and had no existence as a mother goddess. In this sense, she is closely related to Lilith, who is highly sexual, while being completely independent of husbands or children. Inanna's counterpart in Babylonian civilization was the female goddess Ishtar, a similarly powerful female deity.

SCORPION GENITALS

Another type of female demon closely resembling Lilith is Lamashtu, the daughter of the Mesopotamian sky god, Anu. Lamashtu was a highly malevolent demon with a scorpion between her legs instead of genitals, who not only seduced men but would harm pregnant women and newborn babies. She liked to drink blood and to poison living plants. She was often depicted with the head of a lion and bird feet, her breasts suckled by a dog and a pig, riding a donkey. Unlike Lilith, she was ugly and misshapen, yet she still exuded a sexual magnetism that could attract men, as well as repulse them.

SEXUAL REBELLION

There are many fascinating versions of female demons in early Hebrew texts, some of which contradict the creation myth. In one story, the Alphabet of Ben Sira, the storm demon Lilith appears as the first wife of Adam. When Adam demands that she lie beneath him during sexual intercourse, she refuses, saying that God created them both equal. Instead, she demands to lie on top of Adam when they make love. Adam will not concede, and God takes Adam's side, casting her out of the Garden of Eden. She then flies off and consorts with Samael and other demons, producing demonic children, a hundred of whom die every day. In some stories, such as those of the Kabbalah, Lilith herself turns into a serpent. In a fascinating twist to the creation story in Genesis, it is Lilith, in the guise of the serpent, who tempts Eve, Adam's new wife with the apple of knowledge, eventually causing Adam and Eve to be banished from the Garden of Eden.

In the Middle Ages, the myth of the demon Lilith continued. She was believed to have married the king of demons, Asmodeus, spreading chaos and misery at every opportunity. If a man became impotent, or a woman was found to be infertile, or a child died in infancy, Lilith would be blamed. Up until the 18th century, this superstition persisted: a magic circle would be drawn around the bedroom when a mother gave birth, and both mothers and babies would be given amulets to protect them. The names of the three angels who had tried to take Lilith back to Adam — Sanvi, Sansanvi, and Semangelof — would also be invoked to keep her away from the birth chamber. In early times, such misfortunes as infertility or cot deaths were often explained by the destructive influence of Lilith.

DEMON OR GODDESS?

Later, in the Romantic period, the German writer Goethe returned to the subject of Lilith in his great play *Faust*, characterizing her as a sorceress who suffocates men by winding her long hair tightly around them. In the Victorian period, the poet Robert Browning took a different approach, emphasizing that Lilith has an abject attachment to Adam, crawling like a snake to him and promising to be his slave.

In contemporary times, there has been a re-evaluation of Lilith. Some view her as an early mother goddess overseeing and celebrating an essentially feminine sphere of sexuality and fertility, on a par with positive nurturing deities such as the Egyptian goddess Isis. According to this view, the rise of a patriarchal culture emphasized the negative aspects of womanhood, particularly from a sexual point of view, so that instead of being an essentially benevolent female force, the goddess Lilith becomes a destructive demon. Perhaps the most balanced way to view her, from our current perspective, is as a counterpart to such deities as the Indian goddess Kali, who has great sexual power that can be wielded for both positive or negative use. Significantly, this more subtle interpretation links with today's approach to the vampire myth, which stresses the creature's sympathetic, as well as destructive, aspects.

THE LEGACY OF LILITH

The positive aspects of Lilith are emphasized in modern times by feminist thinkers, and by occultists, such as Wiccans and Satanists. Some magical orders, such as the Ordo Antichristianus Illuminati, involve initiations calling on the goddess Lilith. One German rite describes Lilith:

Dark is she, but brilliant. Black are her wings, black on black. Her lips are red as rose, kissing all of the Universe. She is Lilith, who leadeth forth the hordes of the Abyss, and leadeth man to liberation. She is the irresistible fulfiller of all lust, seer of desire. First of all women was she – Lilith, not Eve was the first. Her hand brings forth the revolution of the Will and true freedom of the mind. She is Queen of the Magic. Look on her in lust and despair!

As well as being an important figure in modern occultism, Lilith also appears in popular culture, in various guises. She is a recurring theme in songs by American and European heavy metal bands, and continues to be a perennial source of inspiration in science fiction and fantasy films and literature.

Watercolour painting by Fay Pomerance depicting the demon Lilith with Samael [upon whom she is seated]. The painting is entitled, *The Sixth Palace of Hell*, and relates to the death-bed experience of the evil man.

LAMIA

The playwright Aristophanes claimed that Lamia's name came from the Greek word for gullet, and that she was called this because she had an unpleasant habit of eating small children. Lamia was originally an ancient queen of Libya, the daughter of King Belus of Egypt. She appears in the writings of Diodorus Siculus, a historian writing between 60 and 30 BC. According to him, when Lamia's father died, she became a demon. In some ancient tales, she is seen as the daughter of Poseidon — not the Egyptian King — and therefore has close associations to the sea.

THE CHILD EATER

According to Greek mythology, Lamia had an illicit sexual relationship with the god Zeus, ruler of the Greek pantheon, and bore him several children. This infuriated Zeus' wife Hera so much that she captured Lamia's children and murdered them. Legend has it that, as a result of this horrific experience, Lamia went mad and left her home to wander the earth. Her madness took the form of preying on the children of other women, particularly newborn infants. She would attack them at night, carrying them off to a deserted place and devouring them greedily, in revenge for the crime committed against her.

PRETTY UGLY

Diodorus Siculus wrote that over time, Lamia became a hideous old hag. However, in other versions of the myth, Lamia retains her beauty in the upper half of her body, while in the lower, she grows a penis, which she hides by draping a snakeskin around her loins.

In Roman times, the poet Horace added to the legend by suggesting that the wife of Zeus, Hera, may have actually forced Lamia to eat her own children, rather than simply murdering them. And there is also a suggestion that Hera cursed Lamia with the inability to close her eyes, so that she could find no rest, and was forever unable to dispel the vision of her dead children's faces from her consciousness.

In some versions of the legend, Zeus takes pity on Lamia and gives her the ability to take her eyes out, so that she will be able to rest. According to some sources, this also gives Lamia the gift of prophecy. However, she continues to live a nightmare existence, seemingly unable to stop herself from preying on sleeping infants and stealing them away to drink their blood and eat their flesh.

FEMALE VICE

Over the centuries that followed, the more sympathetic aspect of Lamia's history as a bereaved mother driven to her crimes by madness dropped away, and she became the personification of female vice. Instead of being a single historical figure, her name came to be interchangeable with that of the succubus and the harlot, or indeed any malevolent female figure. She eventually became part of

European folklore, and was feared by men, women and children alike; mothers would threaten their children with the tale of Lamia, telling them that she would come to get them at night if they misbehaved.

....

LAMIA THE ENCHANTRESS

As well as a child eater, Lamia was also feared as a seductress. In the ninth century, the archbishop of Reims listed Lamia as one of the major threats to marriage. Many years later, John Keats revived this notion of Lamia as enchantress in his famous poem of the same name. His verses tell the story of the god Hermes, who sets out to find a nymph whose beauty is legendary. In the process of his search, he meets Lamia, who has been imprisoned in the bodily form of a snake. The snake tells Hermes where to find the nymph, and in return Hermes magically restores Lamia to her human form. Lamia then becomes betrothed to a young man from Corinth called Lycius, but on their wedding day a sage named Apollonius reveals her true identity. The wedding is called off, and Lycius dies of grief. Meanwhile, Hermes and the nymph are united.

Lamia has also proved inspirational to a number of other artists and writers. A famous painting by Herbert Draper in 1909 showed Lamia as a creature with the head and torso of a beautiful young woman, with a snake curling around her arm, and a snakeskin girdle around her waist. She also makes many appearances in popular culture, whether in film, literature, music or video games. Today, she is most often imagined in her guise as half-snake, half-woman, usually striking a seductive pose, and naked from the waist up.

BEHEMOTH

The word behemoth today conjures up any kind of huge, lumbering monster. But in the past it had a more specific meaning, as a primeval beast mentioned in the Old Testament, who later became part of the demon horde categorized by medieval theologians.

CHIEF MONSTER

According to the Book of Job, Behemoth was one of God's first creations, along with Adam the human being. Behemoth was reported to look like a huge hippopotamus or a scaly dragon and to live in a swamp, where he ate grass like an ox. His tail was as big as a cedar tree, and his bones were as strong as brass or bars of iron. His thirst was great, so much so that he could drink the whole of the river Jordan. He was the chief of God's monsters on land, comparable in greatness to Leviathan, the sea monster (see page 21-22), and Ziz, the lord of the sky.

....

CUT UP AND EATEN

According to Jewish scripture, when the end of the world came, Behemoth and Leviathan would fight a great battle for supremacy. The two would finally kill each other, and then their bodies would be cut up and eaten; the same fate would await the other primordial monster of the sky, Ziz. A Jewish hymn recounted how the event would proceed: 'With his horns the Behemoth will gore with strength; the fish (Leviathan) will leap to meet him with his fins, with power. Their Creator will approach them with his mighty sword. From the beautiful skin of the Leviathan, God will construct canopies to shelter the righteous, who will eat the meat of the Behemoth and the Leviathan amid great joy and merriment, at a huge banquet that will be given for them.'

••••

BEHEMOTH THE BUTLER

Like Leviathan, in medieval times Behemoth was characterized not only as a monster, but as an evil demon. According to some demonologists, it was Behemoth rather than Beelzebub who was the prince of gluttony. In other accounts, he is described as the butler and cup bearer of hell, serving at the table of gluttony, lust, sloth and the other deadly sins. The 16th-century priest, Urbain Grandier, who was burned at the stake for practising witchcraft, classified Behemoth as a demon; however, Pierre De Lancre, who led a ruthless witch-hunt during the same period, was convinced that Behemoth was a monster with magical powers, able to transform himself into different animals, including a fox, an elephant, a wolf and a dog.

Behemoth is an important figure in literature through the ages, and makes a memorable appearance in John Milton's 17th-century epic poem, *Paradise Lost*. In it, he describes the animals of creation being born from earth's 'fertile womb', including Behemoth:

Scarce from his mould
Behemoth, biggest born of earth upheaved
His vastness; fleeced the flocks and bleating rose
As plants: ambiguous between sea and land
The river horse, and scaly crocodile

••••

FACT OR FICTION?

Some scholars today suggest that the description of Behemoth that we find in the Bible and other early religious texts is not purely the stuff of legend, but may have some basis in reality. In the Book of Job, Behemoth and Leviathan, are listed among a variety of ordinary animals, such as goats, leading commentators to believe that they may be factual descriptions of animals such as the water buffalo, the elephant, the rhinoceros, the crocodile or the hippopotamus. The observation that the Behemoth's tail 'moves like a cedar', as well as implying great size, could also refer to the swaying of the elephant's trunk. Another interpretation is that the 'cedar' is in fact a polite metaphor for the penis; it is set in 'stones' or testicles, and 'moves' which, in Hebrew, may also mean 'extends'.

The demonic forms of Behemoth and Leviathan from William Blake's *Illustrations to the Book of Job* (1825).

The Last Judgement

by Hieronymus Bosch.

Born around 1450, Bosch spent his entire artistic career in the small Dutch town of Hertogenbosch, from which he derived his surname. At the time of his death in 1516, he was internationally celebrated as an eccentric painter of religious visions who dealt in particular with the torments of hell. None of Bosch's pictures are dated, although the artist signed many of them.

Section Two:

MUTANT MONSTERS

IN MANY CULTURES THERE ARE stories of mutant monsters with hideous, stomach-churning deformities. In Greek mythology there are numerous examples of these monsters: the Cyclops, Centaur and the Gorgons being truly excellent ones. The race of giants known as the cyclopes are enormous brutes, each with a large eye in the middle of its forehead, and a fierce temper. The Centaur is a hybrid creature, with the torso of a strong man, and the lower body of a horse, but the most terrifying of all is perhaps the Gorgons, a trio of winged, female demons. The infamous Medusa and her two sisters, Stheno and Euryale, did not have normal heads of hair, but rather nests of hissing snakes, which could attack at will. Their faces were so incomprehensibly ugly that if human eyes ever fell upon them, the tragic spectator would turn immediately to stone.

CYCLOPS

The Cyclops is one of the most famous monsters of all time. In Greek mythology, the Cyclops was a member of a race of giants, the cyclopes, who only had one eye, which was right in the centre of their foreheads. Myths and legends about these primordial creatures abounded, but all agreed that the giants were a powerful force in human affairs, responsible for disaster, strife, and all manner of harmful events.

ONE-EYED GIANT

As well as the single eye, the giants were known for their massive strength, and also for their vile temper. They were said to have originated from the dark pit of Tartarus, a gloomy dungeon beneath the Underworld. They were the sons of Uranus, the god of the sky, and Gaia, the goddess of the earth. Their main skill was forging iron to make the gods' weapons, such as Poseidon's trident, Artemis' bow and arrow, and Hades' helmet of invisibility, which he gave to Perseus so that the warrior could kill the Gorgon, Medusa.

According to Greek legend, Uranus feared his sons' strength, so he locked the giants in the dungeon of Tartarus for many years, guarded them by a female dragon called Campe. There they worked forging iron, in the sooty blackness. Three of the cyclopes brothers, Arges, Brontes, and Steropes, then set about making thunder claps and lightning for Zeus, which were so powerful that they became Zeus' main weapon of war. In gratitude, Zeus freed the cyclopes, allowing them to roam the earth again, to the consternation of the gods, and, of course, to humanity.

THE MYTH GROWS

Various Greek writers embellished on the myth of the cyclopes, as the race of giants became known. The poet and scholar Callimachus wrote that the cyclopes were the servants of the lame Hephaestus, the god of blacksmiths (known to the Romans as Vulcan), and that the rumbling of volcanoes could be attributed to the sound of the giants working at the forge. In Greek history, many great buildings were said to have been constructed by the cyclopes, including the fortifications of Mycenae in the Peloponnese, which are now an important archeological site. The playwright Euripedes also told the story, in his play Alcestis, of how the sun god Apollo killed the cyclopes because Zeus had angered him by murdering Asclepius, the god of medicine. As a punishment for his crime, Apollo was forced to become the servant of a king.

POLYPHEMUS

The most famous Cyclops in Greek legend was a giant named Polyphemus, whose name means 'much spoken of'. His mother was a sea nymph, Thoosa, and his father was the ruler of the sea, Poseidon. The story of Polyphemus is told in Homer's *Odyssey*, when the hero Odysseus lands on the island where

the cyclopes live, on his way home from the Trojan war. Searching for shelter, Odysseus and 12 of his men find a great cave, where they stay for the night. However, the giant Polyphemus returns, after tending his flocks on the hills, and blocks the entrance to the cave with a large stone, so that the men are trapped. Polyphemus then has two of the men for supper, killing them first by rapping them on the ground.

····

THE FLAMING STAKE

The following day, Polyphemus eats two more of the men for breakfast before going out with his sheep. Knowing that the giant will return and polish off more of his men, Odysseus finds a huge club belonging to Polyphemus, and sharpens it. As expected, Polyphemus returns and eats two more of the men, at which point Odysseus offers him some strong wine. Polyphemus becomes intoxicated and asks Odysseus his name; Odysseus replies that it is 'nobody'. Shortly afterwards, the giant passes out, whereupon Odysseus raises the stake, flaming with fire, and plunges it into his one eye. Polyphemus, blinded and in terrible pain, calls to his brothers that 'nobody' has hurt him, but they do not come to his aid, thinking that he is joking.

The next day, the men tie themselves to the underbellies of the sheep, and the blinded Polyphemus, who feels the back of each sheep to make sure the men are not riding on it, lets them out of the cave. Odysseus and his men manage to get to their ship and sail away, and as they leave, he shouts out his real name. He later regrets this, since Polyphemus asks his father, Poseidon, to send storms at sea, so that Odysseus will have a long and difficult journey home.

POLYPHEMUS THE LOVER

Other stories about Polyphemus show him in a more positive light. The poet Theocritus described him as a gentle, peace-loving shepherd who roams the hills singing, and who falls in love with a sea nymph called Galatea. In Virgil's *Aeneid*, after having been blinded, Polyphemus rushes down to the sea to bathe his wounded eye, crying out in pain as he does so. Aeneas, the hero of the tale, manages to escape, and Polyphemus is left howling for help. Alerted by his cries, the other cyclopes run to the seashore, but they can only watch helplessly as the ship sails off to the horizon.

Many years later, the Roman poet Ovid wrote an amusing story called *Acis and Galatea*. This imagined the love story between Polyphemus and the sea nymph in more detail. In Ovid's recounting of the tale, Polyphemus kills another suitor of Galatea's, Acis, with a boulder. He then tries to make himself attractive to the nymph, trimming his beard and writing her a poem. Galatea, of course, is not interested in the oafish cannibal Polyphemus, so it is with a mixture of humour and pathos that Ovid imagines the giant's doomed infatuation.

The story of the Cyclops Polyphemus continued to fascinate writers, musicians and artists in the centuries that followed. The painter Nicholas Poussin and the sculptor August Rodin both immortalized him, and he was also the subject of an opera by the French composer, Jean Cras.

···················

CYCLOPS THE X-MAN

In the 20th century, Cyclops became a favourite in the Marvel Comics Universe, where he was the leader of the X-men superheroes team. In this incarnation, he is able to emit an 'optic blast' from his battle visor, which has a single ruby 'eye' at its centre. The human form of Cyclops is Scott Summers, who is recruited by Professor Charles Xavier to lead the X-men, whose mission it is to create a world in which mutants and humans can live in harmony.

In many ways, Scott Summers embodies the traditional values of the American dream. He has a close and dutiful relationship with the professor, a father figure, before emerging as the leader of the X-men. Instead of being rebellious and individualist like some in his team, such as Wolverine (whose motto is 'I go where I wanna go'), Summers/Cyclops is very disciplined and moral. He is also highly skilled, with formidable abilities as a leader, strategist and technician. In this, he shows very little connection with his ancestor, the lumbering, slow-witted Cyclops of Ancient Greek mythology; only the single eye, radiating from Summers' battle visor, reminds us of the legend of the doomed race of giants in classical antiquity.

A Gallo-Roman funerary mask of a bearded cyclops. Musée de la Civilisation Gallo-Romaine, Lyon.

BASILISK

The Basilisk is a mythical beast who is thought to be king of the snake world and able to cause death to a victim simply by looking at him. As no one has ever encountered the monstrous creature and lived to tell the tale, accounts vary of his appearance.

KING OF THE SNAKES

In European legend, the Basilisk is a small reptilian creature; indeed, his name comes from the Greek word for 'little king'. In medieval times, he was often depicted on family crests and shields, where he appeared as an animal with the body, head, and legs of a cockerel, and the tail of a snake. Sometimes his wings were feathered; alternatively, they were shown as being covered in scales. He has a crown-shaped white spot in the shape of a crest, diadem or mitre on his head, to show that he is king of the snakes. As well as in heraldry, the Basilisk can be found in stone carvings on buildings and in churches from this period.

As well as this half-bird, half-serpent body, the Basilisk has many other curious features. The Ancient Greeks conceived of it as a small snake that left a trail of poisonous venom in its wake; in addition, it emitted a foul stench. The creature was believed to be the offspring of a cockerel and the egg of a serpent or toad. Instead of slithering along on the ground like a normal snake, the Basilisk was able to stand, maintaining an upright position as it moved along. In some images of the Basilisk, it had no legs; in others, it had short legs with clawed feet, like a bird.

DEADLY POISON

The Roman writer Pliny the Elder describes how, as the Basilisk passes, all the vegetation in the area is scorched as if by fire. Not only this, but if a person tried to attack it with a spear, the poison will run up the spear and kill them. In his encyclopaedia, written in AD 79, Pliny went on to explain how the Basilisk could be dealt with:

> To this dreadful monster the effluvium of the weasel is fatal, a thing that has been tried with success, for kings have often desired to see its body when killed; so true is it that it has pleased Nature that there should be nothing without its antidote. The animal is thrown into the hole of the Basilisk, which is easily known from the soil around it being infected. The weasel destroys the Basilisk by its odour, but dies itself in this struggle of nature against its own self.

In the Middle Ages, the legend of the Basilisk grew, with stories that the beast could kill victims simply by breathing on them. The English monk known as The Venerable Bede stated that, in addition to the cockerel fertilizing the egg of the snake or toad to create the Basilisk, the astrological conditions must be right — with Sirius rising. The Basilisk was also connected to theories about alchemy, with magicians claiming that they could convert copper or silver into gold by using the ashes of a dead Basilisk in their spells. The Basilisk also became linked to another mythical creature, the cockatrice, a type of dragon with a cock's head. The cockatrice was believed to be conceived from an egg laid by a cock (which is impossible) and incubated by a toad or snake. This was an inversion of the Basilisk story, in which the egg is laid by the snake and fertilized by the cock. Eventually, in some retellings of the story, the two creatures, the Basilisk and the cockatrice, became the same monster; in Chaucer's *Canterbury Tales*, a 'basilicok' is mentioned.

....

MIRRORS & COCK CROWS

As the centuries passed, the legend of the Basilisk grew. It became a great beast, and was reputed to be able to breathe flames. It could kill victims merely by the sound of its voice; it could also poison someone by touching an inanimate object which the person then touched. Some believed the Basilisk would die if it saw its hideous form in a mirror, or if it heard the crow of a cock in the morning. Medieval travellers sometimes carried a cockerel with them, to ward off this fearsome creature. They might also take mirrors to defend themselves, since the Polish legend of the Basilisk of Warsaw recounted how the monster was killed by a man who carried with him a set of mirrors.

Today, the Basilisk is the symbol of the city of Basel, in Switzerland. In former times, the Basilisk was shown holding the heraldic shield of the city, which features a crozier; today, the image has been simplified, so that only the shield remains. However, the ancient Basilisk still appears on old buildings and monuments in the city.

....

THE MONGOOSE & THE COBRA

In modern times, speculation continues as to whether the legend of the Basilisk has any basis in reality. Some believe that Eu-ropeans may have heard stories about the cobra and its enemy the mongoose from travellers to the East. Like the Basilisk, who moves in an upright, erect fashion rather than slithering on its belly, the cobra is able to stand, raising its front part. In addition, some species of cobra have a crown-like structure on the head, and are able to numb or temporarily blind victims by spitting at them. Moreover, in eastern countries, the mongoose is often used to kill snakes, which may have helped to give rise to the European legend of the Basilisk, a creature who embodies aspects of both these animals.

....

THE LEGEND LIVES ON

Basilisks have been a popular symbol among many writers and artists, including poets and painters, who have used them literally or figuratively to describe terrifying powers, such as the ability to kill with a look, and also with extreme ugliness and disgusting behaviour. Most recently, Basilisks have appeared in fantasy and science fiction, as well as role-playing games. The Basilisk is also featured as a monstrous beast in the Harry Potter series of novels by J.K. Rowling. In *Harry Potter and the Chamber of Secrets*, the Basilisk lurks inside a dark chamber, a terrifying green snake whose stare can cause instant death. In order to avoid this fate, the Basilisk must be viewed through a mirror, or as a reflection in water. In this case, the viewer will be turned to stone rather than killed, and can only be restored by drinking a special potion made from a mandrake. In cases of poisoning, the tears of a phoenix must be used as an antidote. Nothing other than this rare cure will be effective.

Rowling also discusses the Basilisk in her book *Fantastic Beasts and Where to Find*

Them, in which she describes the legendary creature as a massive green snake, up to 50ft (15m) long, created by a wizard named Herpo the Foul, who used a toad to hatch a chicken's egg. The only way a Basilisk can be subdued is by talking to it in 'Parseltongue', the language of serpents that only a few human beings, such as Harry Potter himself, can speak.

Today, as well as in fantasy fiction, the term Basilisk appears in zoology to denote a particular type of South American lizard.

GRENDEL

The legendary monster Grendel appears in one of the most important works of Anglo-Saxon literature, the epic poem *Beowulf*, which was written in Old English some time between AD 700 and the year 1000. The poem tells the story of the hero, Beowulf, a brave warrior, who protects his people from a number of threats, including a terrible dragon, and a troll-like monster known as Grendel. Beowulf kills Grendel, and also Grendel's mother, another monster who is equally ferocious.

SON OF THE SERPENT

In *Beowulf*, Grendel the monster is described as a descendent of Cain, the evil brother in the story of Cain and Abel, that comes from the Hebrew bible. Cain and Abel were the sons of Adam and Eve, though some interpreters believe that Cain was a direct son of the serpent in the creation story told in the book of Genesis. Cain is a crop farmer, while his brother Abel is a shepherd. In the biblical story, Cain kills Abel out of jealousy when God rejects his sacrifice of gifts that he has grown, preferring to accept Abel's sacrifice of animals.

....

KILLING AND EATING

In the story of Beowulf, the great warrior leaves his home in Geatland, Sweden, the traditional home of the Goth tribe, in order to hunt down the monster Grendel. Grendel has been making attacks on the great hall of Heorot, where the king conducts his feasts and banquets. In the poem, Heorot, which means, 'hall of the hart', is described as 'the foremost of halls under heaven'. Grendel kills and eats anyone he finds in the great hall, and none can escape him.

It is unclear from the poem why Grendel makes these attacks, but many later retellings of the story recount how Grendel is angered by the drunken merriment of the warriors as they feast, and enters the great hall to punish the revellers for disturbing him from his sleep. Beowulf waits for him, and when Grendel appears, begins to fight him. After a great struggle, Beowulf manages to cut Grendel's arm off with his sword. Grendel is so badly wounded that he retreats to his cave in the swamp, where he dies.

....

BLOOD REVENGE

The following night, Grendel's mother appears at the great hall, seeking to avenge the murder of her son. According to the law of the times, known as 'weregild', she had a right to take revenge for a member of her family who had been killed — this was known as 'blood revenge'. In her pursuit of Beowulf, Grendel's mother starts slaying the sleeping warriors. When Beowulf learns what has happened in the great hall, he goes back to the swamp and finds her there. The two of them engage in battle, beside the corpse of Grendel, and eventually, with the help of a giant enchanted sword, Beowulf manages to triumph. He decapitates Grendel's mother, and then takes the head off Grendel's corpse, and keeps it as a trophy. On his return to the great hall, the king, named Hroogar, the queen, Wealthow, and all the warriors celebrate by showering gifts on him, such as gold and horses, and they compose a special poem for him, telling of his great deeds, which they sing to him.

....

THE GIANT GOES BERSERK

The author of *The Lord of the Rings*, J.R.R. Tolkein, was one of the first writers to popularize the story of Beowulf, which up to that time had been very much the province of Anglo-Saxon scholars. He focused on the nature of Grendel, the mother, and a great dragon, who is Beowulf's final opponent in the story. Today, Grendel is often depicted as a Neanderthal giant, but in actual fact, there is very little detailed description of what the monster looks like in the original poem, beyond that he is a very large creature. The poet Seamus Heaney, in a famous translation of the poem, says that Grendel has the warped shape of a man but is 'an unnatural birth'; he describes Grendel's severed arm:

Every nail, claw-scale and spur, every spike
and welt on the hand of that heathen brute
was like barbed steel. Everybody said
there was no honed iron hard enough
to pierce him through, no time proofed blade
that could cut his brutal blood-caked claw...

However, some scholars believe that Grendel was not humanoid in shape, but might have been a dragon that walked on two feet. Others believe that Grendel might have been a human warrior, called a 'Berserker'. Berserkers were soldiers who went into battle in a state of complete fury, almost like a trance. There are various ideas as to how they got into this state; it may be that they took hallucinatory drugs prior to going into battle, possibly eating them in food, to give them strength and courage; or it could simply have been a kind of spiritual fervour that impelled them. Whatever the case, the berserkers were legendary for their brutality, giving rise to the modern term 'going berserk', when a person loses all sense of self-control and allows a manic fit of rage to overcome them, often leading to violence and destruction.

....

GRENDEL TODAY

The legend of Grendel continues today, with numerous book and film adaptations, including a novel of the same name by American writer John Gardner, who retold the story from the monster's point of view. The novel was illustrated with woodcuts by Emil Antonucci, showing abstract images of the monster's head. A decade after it was published, there was a film adaptation, an animated movie named 'Grendel Grendel

GRENDEL

Grendel'. The film starred Peter Ustinov as the voice of the monster. In the film, Grendel appears as thoughtful and sensitive at times, but suddenly seized by the urge to be violent.

There is also a long-running series of comic books by the same name; the author, Matt Wagner, has called the series, 'a study of the nature of aggression'.

Grendel abducting and devouring young men from the myth of Beowulf.

A Centaur fighting from 13th century Italian bestiary fresco. San Giacomo in Castella Bolzano, Italy.

CENTAUR

In Greek mythology, there exists a creature with the torso of a man and the body of a horse. The centaurs were believed to be closely linked to Dionysus, the god of wine, revelry and pleasure. They lived on wine and meat, and were reputed to have a brutal, violent nature. As well as gorging their appetites, they were also very lustful, and were said to carry off young women for sex. In a sense, they embodied the dual nature of humanity: both rational and sensual, intelligent and bestial.

WILD HORSEMEN

The centaurs were said to be the offspring of a king named Ixion, ruler of the Lapiths, an ancient tribe from Thessaly. Ixion went mad and was deposed as king, whereupon Zeus brought him to Mount Olympus. Ixion then fell in love with Hera, Zeus' wife. Suspicious of Ixion's motives, Zeus fashioned a woman that looked exactly like Hera out of clouds. He named the cloud nymph Nephele, and laid her down next to Ixion while he was asleep. When Ixion awoke, he found the naked Nephele beside him, and they began to make love. Furious, Zeus sent a thunderbolt

Mosaic from the 2nd century AD depicting centaurs at a lion hunt.

down from heaven, and condemned Ixion to be bound to a burning wheel, circling the heavens, for ever.

Nephele, the cloud nymph, went on to bear a child as a result of her union with Ixion. It was a hunched, deformed infant, and she called it Centaurus. The boy grew up in the mountains, where he roamed wild with the horses there, mating with them. In this way, he sired the race known as the centaurs. The centaurs were said to inhabit the various regions of Greece, including Mount Pelion in Thessaly.

Over time, the wild centaurs began to fight with the Lapith tribe, ironically enough, since they were related to them through King Ixion. Typically, they would attack the humans by throwing rocks at them, uprooting trees, and using the branches as weapons. They behaved like untamed horses, but they did have a human side: in this sense, they stood as a powerful image of the struggle between barbarism and civilization.

Some believe that the myth of the centaur arose when tribes who knew nothing of riding first saw nomads mounted on horses. To them, the riders would have seemed like beasts who were half human and half animal. It is thought that the Lapiths brought horse riding to Greece: certainly, many Greek writers described the Lapiths as being the original horsemen of the country, and the tribes themselves boasted that their horses were descended from the centaur race.

PINDAR'S CENTAUR

The first written mention of centaurs comes in the work of the poet Pindar, who describes the monsters' hybrid nature. Centaurs went on to have great significance in Roman civilization, where they were often shown drawing chariots. However, the poet Lucretius cast doubt on their existence, pointing out

that the lifespan of humans is much longer than that of horses, which would make such a hybrid impossible. Over the centuries, scholars have had many different theories as to where the centaurs originated. Some, such as Robert Graves, believed that they were originally part of Indian mythology, where early sculptures show the half-man, half-horse image, which may have been worshipped as a totem.

····

FEMALE CENTAURS

Female centaur, or centaurides, are mentioned in Greek literature as the sisters and wives of the centaurs. The Greek thinker Philostratus described the centaurides:

Some grow out of white mares, others are attached to chestnut mares, and the coats of others are dappled, but they glisten like those of horses that are well cared for. There is also a white female centaur that grows out of a black mare, and the very opposition of the colours helps to produce the united beauty of the whole.

····

THE 'POLKAN'

The legend of the centaur continued during the Middle Ages, where they were depicted as ploughboys riding goats, or as demons plaguing saints on their travels. In Russian folk art, a similar figure called the 'polkan' exists, a half-human, half-horse or dog, that possesses great power and speed. In modern times, the centaur has been represented sympathetically, for example by C.S. Lewis in *The Chronicles of Narnia* series, and by J.K. Rowling in her *Harry Potter* novels. This follows the Greek tradition in which one leading centaur, Chiron, was said to have a more refined nature than his brothers, being sired from a different lineage which made him kind, wise and clever.

CERBERUS

Cerberus is the guardian of the gates of the Underworld. His job is to prevent dead souls who have crossed the river Styx — the passage from earth to hell — from escaping and also to stop the living from entering. His terrifying appearance, with his dragon's body, hissing snake-heads covering his back like hair, and numerous angry heads sprouting from his neck, would strike fear into those attempting to pass through the gates of hell.

THE SHE-VIPER'S SON

It is thought that the name 'Cerberus' might be linked to the Sanskrit 'Sarvara', which describes the dogs belonging to the Lord of Death, Yama, a Buddhist and Hindu deity. In Greek legend, Cerberus is believed to be a brother to many other famous monsters, such as the Sphinx (a creature with a lion's body and a human head), the Hydra (a multi-headed, subterranean serpent), the Ladon (a dragon-like snake), the Chimera (a fire-breathing monster made up of various animal parts), and the Nemean Lion (a vicious beast known for its extreme violence). In most cases these monsters are composite beings, who not only have extraordinary powers, but also display an insatiable appetite for killing.

Cerberus was believed to have been conceived by Typhon, a giant who breathed fire, whom the gods feared greatly, and a creature called Echidna, known as the 'she-viper'. Echidna was half-serpent, half-woman, and was said to be the mother of all monsters. The Greek oral poet, Hesiod described her:

Half a nymph with glancing eyes and fair cheeks, and half again a huge snake, great and awful, with speckled skin, eating raw flesh beneath the secret parts of the holy earth. And there she has a cave deep down under a hollow rock far from the deathless gods and mortal men... grim Echidna, a nymph who dies not nor grows old all her days.

THE THREE HEADS

Echidna's son Cerberus inherited her lust for raw meat, preferably of live humans or animals, which allowed the spirits of the dead to come into the Underworld, but not to leave it. Cerberus' brother was said to be Orthrus, a two-headed monster who guarded a herd of red-skinned cattle belonging to a giant, Geryon. In some versions of the Greek myth, it is Orthrus rather than Typhon that impregnates Echidna, giving rise to the fearsome brood of monsters such as Cerberus, the Chimera, the Hydra and the Sphinx.

The meaning of Cerberus' three heads has been interpreted by poets and artists in several ways. According to some sources, the three heads denote, birth, youth and old age; others claim that each of the heads can see into the present, the past and the future. In most versions of the legend, Cerberus has as his master the god of the Underworld, Hades (who, in Roman times, came to be known as Pluto). Hades was both the name of the ruler of the Underworld, and of the Underworld itself.

HERACLES

There are many tales in Greek legend as to how Cerberus could be outwitted and overcome. In the story of the Labours of Heracles, the hero manages to defeat Cerberus without weapons, as demanded, slinging the great hound over his back and taking him out of the Underworld through a cave. When Heracles brings Cerberus before King Eurystheus of Mycenae, whom he is bound to serve, the king is so terrified that he asks Heracles to take it back to hell. Heracles is then released from his labours, a series of tasks that he had been compelled to perform to gain his freedom. In other stories, Cerberus is drugged so that the hero can creep past him back to the world of the living; for example, in the *Aeneid*, the hound is given honeycakes which contain a sleeping potion. In another episode, Orpheus manages to lull Cerberus into a deep sleep by playing him music.

The legend of Cerberus continues in Western art and literature, most memorably in Dante's *Inferno*, where he appears as a giant worm in the third circle of hell, devouring those who have committed the sin of gluttony, and in John Milton's *Paradise Lost*, which tells of 'Cerberean' hell hounds that never stop barking.

THE GORGONS

The Gorgons were three winged female demons in ancient Greek mythology. They had snakes for hair, and faces so hideous that they turned all who looked at them to stone. They were sisters named Medusa, Stheno and Euryale; daughters of the sea god Phorcys and his wife Ceto, a sea monster. As well as their hissing hair, the Gorgons had wide, staring eyes, lolling tongues, large nostrils, and tusks like those of pigs. The word 'gorgos' in Greek means 'dreadful', and it is from this word that the trio of demonic hags were named.

MEDUSA

The most infamous of the Gorgons was Medusa, who was a mortal, unlike her two sisters. According to legend, King Polydectes, ruler of the island of Seriphos, sent the warrior Perseus to kill Medusa, armed with a sharp, curved sword, winged boots, and a cloak that rendered him invisible. Perseus also carried a mirrored shield given to him by the goddess Athena, so that he could cut off the monster's head without looking at her and being turned to stone. This he did, decapitating her with his sword; but as she died, blood dripped from her neck, and out of it sprang her two sons by the sea god Poseidon, Pegasus the winged horse, and his brother Chrysaor.

There are many stories about what

Gorgons of the Secession. Sculptures over the doors of the Secession Art Museum in Vienna, Austria. The masks of the three gorgons preside over the entrance symbolizing the three art forms – architecture, sculpture and painting. The Secession also houses Gustav Kilmt's famous *Beethoven Frieze*.

happened to Medusa's head after it was cut off. In one version, when Perseus returns to the court of King Polydectes at Sephiros, he holds up the head, to show how he has triumphed. In so doing, he turns the entire court to stone. In another, the divine hero Heracles uses a lock of Medusa's hair to protect a city from attack. Exactly where the Gorgons lived is also open to interpretation, some sources placing their abode as the Gorgades, islands that may now correspond to Cape Verde, the archipelago off the coast of Western Africa.

.....

BEAUTY OR BEAST?

In later myths, Medusa is portrayed as a beautiful woman who is turned into a monster as a punishment for making love with Poseidon. The Roman poet Ovid wrote that Poseidon had been aroused by the beauty of Medusa's hair, and so the goddess Athena (or Minerva, as she was to the Romans) turned her hair into snakes.

Strange tales as to the true nature of the Gorgons abounded, with some poets such as Hesiod characterizing them as demons who guarded rocky reefs under the sea. These, of course, were highly dangerous to shipping. The reefs themselves were often thought of as having been created by Perseus when he laid down Medusa's head, and when, during the attack, he killed a deadly sea monster by turning it to stone. The Gorgons were also thought by some Greek communities to be storm demons, able to whip up fierce winds and to drown sailors at sea should the sailors offend them in any way.

....

WARDING OFF EVIL

Because of their special power, to turn those who looked at them to stone, images of the Gorgons were often put on buildings such as temples, to keep away evil spirits. One

famous example is a stone Gorgon carved at the pediment of a temple in Corfu, thought to be the oldest of its kind in Greece, dating from 600 BC. Other carvings from the period show the Gorgons as having horns, fangs and snake-like skin, or with wings and claws like a bird. These images correspond closely to other figures in Greek mythology, such as the sphinx, and to protective divinities in different cultures, such as the Hindu goddess Kali, who is often shown with a lolling tongue and a snake around her neck. Similarly grotesque faces, with bulging eyes and fangs, have been found on shields used by Chinese soldiers in early times.

Today, it is thought that the legend of the three Gorgons was devised by the poet Hesiod in around 700 BC, and that before that, the Ancient Greeks believed in one goat-like deity, the daughter of a sun god, who was killed by Zeus and made into a shield for him to use in battle. It was believed that the blood of the Gorgon, if taken from the right side, could revive the dead, while the blood from the left side was poisonous, and would cause instant death.

58

Perseus and the Gorgons (*Stheno, Euryale and Medusa*), Walter Crane (1845–1915). Perseus has cut off and is holding Medusa's head.

OGRE

An ogre is a type of monster, smaller than a giant, but much larger than a human being. In appearance, it is like a primitive or Neanderthal humanoid, with a large head, a bushy beard and a great deal of long, wild hair. The ogre has a strong body, often with a fat belly, and a big appetite for human flesh. Characteristically, the ogre is violent and greedy, lacking kindness, mercy or any real human emotion.

THE LAND OF OGRES

The ogre first appears in *Perceval*, a romance poem by Chretien de Troyes, written in the 12th century. In the story, de Troyes refers to 'the land of ogres'. Some believe that de Troyes was referring to Great Britain, as described by Geoffrey of Monmouth, who wrote a popular book called *The History of the Kings of Britain* in the same period. According to Geoffrey, ogres inhabited Britain before it was settled by human beings. A warrior named Corineus, along with a band of Trojans, invaded Albion (as it was then called) and found a number of giants living there. Among these was 'a detestable monster named Gogmagog, in stature 12 cubits, and of such prodigious strength that at one shake he pulled up an oak as if it had been a hazel wand'. (A cubit is thought to have been about one and a half feet.) Geoffrey tells how Corineus managed to defeat Gogmagog, wrestling with him, and eventually managing to throw him over a high cliff to his death.

THE FAIRY TALE ORGE

In 17th-century France, the writer Charles Perrault dedicated his retirement to penning stories for his children, collecting them in a book with the title *Tales of Mother Goose*. This collection became extremely popular, marking the beginning of a new literary genre, the fairy tale. Many of his stories featured a fearsome giant called an ogre; and in his version of Sleeping Beauty, he also mentions a female ogre, or ogress. Another French writer of the period, the Countess d'Aulnoy, also told of ogres in a fairy tale called *The Bee and the Orange Tree*. In the story, a baby princess named Aimee is shipwrecked, her cradle drifting to a land of ogres. She grows up among the ogres, and is due to marry one of them, but falls in love with a shipwrecked man whom she hides in a cave. Eventually, the pair manage to escape by magically turning themselves into various forms, including a bee and an orange tree. The story ends, as all fairy tales should, happily ever after, with the princess marrying her prince.

TROLLS AND ORCS

Closely related to the ogre, in Scandinavian folklore, is the troll. Trolls are ugly, humanoid creatures who live in isolated mountains or caves, and are usually bad-tempered and dim-witted. They are rarely friendly, and may even try to eat human beings. They usually live alone, but sometimes with a single son or daughter. According to legend, trolls can be frightened away by lightning, and are said to be turned to stone if they come into contact with sunlight.

The word 'ogre' is also connected to the Latin *orcus*, and the Old English *orcneas*, which may have provided the inspiration for the writer J.R.R. Tolkien's fictitious warrior race, the orcs. These brutal creatures have grotesque features, and slimy, greenish skin. Since Tolkien's time, orcs have become extremely popular figures in contemporary science fiction and fantasy literature, as well as role play and computer games.

A child-eating ogre, 1520.

THE DRAGON

The dragon is one of the most celebrated mythical creatures of all time. In European culture, it is usually depicted as a huge, reptilian creature with a long body, greenish scales, spikes running down its back, a muscular tail, and short legs with huge claws like those of a lion. However, in the East, it is usually shown as a type of snake, with no wings or legs. Typically, it is said to breathe fire, and in some variants of the myth, its breath, or bite, is believed to be fatal.

EAST MEETS WEST

Symbols and stories of the dragon are found in many countries and cultures across the world: there is a long tradition of tales about dragons in Europe, and another equally ancient one that developed in China and the Far East.

In the European tradition, the dragon is usually seen as an adversary, to be slain by an avenging hero. In most tales, the dragon will guard a castle or treasure, and the hero's task or quest will be to overpower it. In Asian stories, however, the dragon is conceived of differently, often as a wise and supernatural being who may be evil or good, but who will be able to advise humans about important matters in their lives.

These traditions are quite separate, but over time, they have probably influenced each other, so that today, our concept of the dragon draws from each. Dragons in European mythology are usually portrayed as evil, although there are remarkable examples of 'good' dragons in Welsh folklore. The national flag of Wales today consists of a red dragon, and is thought to date back in history to the legendary King Arthur, and other Celtic leaders, who used it as a standard in battle.

THE WYVERN

In early European times, dragons were portrayed as having leathery wings like a bat, and only one pair of legs. These dragons were known as 'wyverns', and were used on heraldic coats of arms, many of which are still used today. There is a school of thought that wyverns may have been based on the winged lizards known as pterosaurs, which died out 65 million years ago. Today, in the West, we mostly encounter dragons when they are used as plot devices in books and films, and usually they are portrayed as huge, fierce creatures.

GUARDING TREASURE

In Western stories, according to folklore, the dragon likes to live in a cave, where, from a young age, it learns to store precious objects. Dragons love gold coins and beautiful jewels, which they may grade into piles, and polish carefully so that they are in good condition. Naturally, the dragons will guard their horde fiercely, and will kill any thieves who attempt to steal it.

HAPPILY EVER AFTER

Dragons usually live alone, but in the mating season, the female dragon makes a distinctive call to attract suitors, and then flies fast and high, in a spectacular demonstration of her prowess. The male dragon will then try to catch her, mounting her as they fall to the ground. Once mated, the pair will then build a nest made of branches, with a lining of gold coins. The dragons breathe on these coins to warm up the nest. The female will then lay her eggs, taking up to two years to do so. Once the eggs are laid, the male and the female take turns to sit on them, the other foraging for food, which consists of wild animals. One way to recognize a dragon's lair is by the pile of bones that lies beside it.

RAVENOUS WYRMLINGS

The baby dragons have a long 'egg tooth', which they use to break out of the hard shell of their eggs. The hatchlings are very hungry, and must be fed immediately on fresh meat, or they will try to eat their siblings. These little creatures then grow into 'wyrmlings' with rows of razor-sharp teeth that can tear meat easily. Their scales, however, remain soft, later hardening into a protective casing for the skin. The wings also remain underdeveloped for some time. Over the next 150 years, reputedly the average lifespan of a dragon, the wyrmlings will grow into dragonets, and then into dragons, reaching a huge height, and growing horns, spines, and wings that will eventually enable them to fly.

As a fully-fledged adult, the dragon will leave home and seek a cave of its own, preferably in a mountainous, isolated place. The dragon will mark its territory by spitting on the rocks and trees around it, so that other dragons can smell its presence. It will seek out an older dragon to learn magic, and will begin to respond to the mating call. After mating, it will form a pair, make a nest and raise the next generation. Legend has it that at the end of the dragon's life, the clan will gather at the edge of a volcano and howl a song known as 'the passing song'. Then the dying dragon will climb to the top of the volcano and hurl itself down into the vortex.

HERACLES AND HYDRA

One of the earliest, and most fearsome, accounts of the dragon is that of the Lernaean Hydra, from Greek myth. This dragon from the underworld breathed deadly fire, and had six to nine heads, one of which was said to be immortal. It was one of the labours of the divine hero Heracles to kill this terrifying dragon, who lived in a remote cave. Heracles did this by shooting burning arrows into the cave, forcing the creature to emerge. The dragon attempted to crush him, coiling itself around him. Each time Heracles cut off one of its heads, a new one would grow in its place. Heracles called for help from his friend Iolaus, who cauterized the stumps of the heads with a torch, preventing the new ones from growing. Heracles then proceeded to kill the dragon, cutting off the immortal head and burying it under a rock by a roadside. Afterwards, he cut open the body of the dragon and dipped his arrows into it, so that they would be lethal to his opponents.

ST GEORGE

Another famous dragon legend in the European tradition dates from the 11th century. St George, who later became the patron saint of England, was a Christian soldier known for his extraordinary courage in battle. He travelled to many countries and, in one instance, happened to be passing a city where a dragon was terrorizing the inhabitants. The dragon had made its nest by a spring that provided water for the city. In order to col-

lect the water, the citizens had to offer the dragon a sheep; and once the sheep ran out, they had to offer a maiden. The unfortunate victim was chosen by drawing lots.

Eventually, the princess of the city's royal family was chosen. Her father, the king, pleaded on her behalf, but to no avail. She was offered to the dragon, but as she faced her death, St George intervened. He made the sign of the cross and then rode forward on his horse, slaying the dragon with his lance, named Ascalon, and rescuing the princess. As a result, the entire population of the city abandoned their pagan religion and converted to Christianity.

THE DRAGON FÁFNIR

This dragon story comes from Norse mythology, and tells the tale of an aggressive dwarf, Fáfnir, who got his hands on his father's hoard of gold and precious gems. He then went into the wilderness, where he turned into a dragon so he could guard his ill-gotten treasure, symbolizing the fate of a greedy person. Fáfnir poisoned the land around his treasure so that no one would be brave enough to come near it.

Eventually, a plan was made to recover the stolen treasure. Fáfnir's brother Regin sent a heroic fighter named Sigurd to fight and kill the dragon, advising him to dig a pit along the path where the dragon crawled to drink water from a stream, so that he could plunge his sword, Gram, into the dragon's underbelly. The god Odin also advised Sigurd, telling him to dig another trench that would hold the dragon's blood. Sigurd managed to pull off the stunt, stabbing Fáfnir in the shoulder and mortally wounding him.

As the dragon lay dying, he predicted that Regin would try to kill Sigurd, since all who got their hands on the treasure immediately became corrupted by greed, as he himself had been. When the dragon finally died, Sigurd cooked his heart, drank his blood, and thereby learned how to understand the language of the birds. The birds told him that Regin was planning to kill him, so in

The nine dragon screen wall, Beijing. Built in 1417, this famous relief is glazed with tiles; depicting nine dragons chasing a pearl in the clouds above the waves.

self-defence, Sigurd responded by cornering Regin and cutting off his his head. Sigurd then ate some of Fáfnir's heart, keeping a portion to give to his wife Gudrun at their marriage.

JÖRMUNGANDR

Another classic Norse myth tells of the serpent Jörmungandr, a dragon-like sea serpent whose father is a god, Loki, and whose mother is a giant, Angrboda. At his birth, the god Odin took Jörmungandr and threw him into the sea surrounding Midgard, or middle earth, the home of human beings, and one of several worlds described in Norse legend. Jörmungandr eventually grew so big that he was able to encircle the earth and grasp his own tail.

The legend claims that if Jörmungandr ever lets go, middle earth will fall apart, and the world will end. A great battle called Ragnarok will take place, in which many gods will be killed. Jörmungandr will come out of the sea and poison the sky, before being slain by the god Thor, his arch enemy. Thor himself will walk nine paces before falling dead, having been poisoned by the bite of the dragon.

BLOODTHIRSTY BATTLE

One of the most bloodthirsty stories about Jörmungandr concerns an episode when the god Thor goes fishing. Thor and his friend, the giant Hymir, prepare a strong line and bait, which Jörmungandr takes. When the line is pulled up and the monstrous dragon is revealed, dripping poisonous blood, Thor grabs a hammer to kill him. Hymir, however, cuts the line and the dragon returns to the deep. This scene was used as the basis for many carvings and paintings, showing that the myth was an important one lasting for around five centuries.

THE EASTERN DRAGON

The Eastern dragon also has a very detailed mythology surrounding it, as well as a variety of fascinating myths. The Chinese imperial dragon, known as 'lung', is thought of as a benevolent spirit, along with the phoenix, the tortoise and the unicorn. The Chinese imperial dragon symbolized the power and might of the Chinese emperors, who were often said to have the features of a dragon, such as a dragon tail. In addition to this, some emperors were suspected to have been fathered by a dragon.

The Chinese dragon is said to be made up of many different animals, including: the camel, which forms the head; the carp, which lends its scales; the horns, from the deer; the eyes, from the hare; the ears, from the bull; the neck, from the snake; the belly, from the clam; the paws, from the tiger; and the claws, from the eagle. There are also four types of dragon: the celestial, protecting the homeland of the gods; the spiritual, controlling the wind and rain; the earth, supervising rivers and seas; and the underworld, guarding precious metals.

In contrast to the evil, greedy European dragon, the Chinese dragon symbolizes potency, strength, and good luck, as well as control over natural elements such as rainfall and wind, avoiding floods and hurricanes. In everyday language, Chinese people speak of a brave person being 'a dragon'. Throughout the East, and especially Japanese and Thai culture, the dragon is esteemed as a powerful supernatural force, sometimes for good, but also, in some instances, for evil.

In the Chinese lunar calendar, 2012 is the year of the dragon. The dragon is said to bring wealth and good-fortune with it and can signify a baby boom across Asia.

WEREWOLF

The werewolf is one of our most intriguing and enduring monsters. Part animal, part human, and liable to change shape at any given moment, the werewolf has been part of European mythology since ancient times, and continues to fascinate and frighten new generations today, as a leading horror figure across many mediums.

....

AN ENDURING MONSTER

The story of the werewolf occurs in humanity's earliest history. In Greek mythology, it appears in the tale of King Lycaon, who cruelly sacrificed a human child to the god Zeus. As a punishment for such a bloodthirsty act of violence, Zeus turned King Lycaon into a wolf. Today, the king's name, Lycaon, is the origin of the term lycanthropy, meaning the process of turning into a wolf, or more recently a mental illness in which the sufferer believes him or herself to be a wolf (or similar kind of animal). The Greek myths and legends, reported by both Greek and Roman poets, also told of a tribe, the Neuri, whose members turned into wolves once a year, for a few days, and then reverted back into humans.

....

ANCIENT ROME

The werewolf cult continued under the Romans, who used the word 'versipellis' to describe the way an individual could change between human and animal forms, as a shape-shifter. One story told of a man who hung his clothes on a tree and went for a swim in a lake, and was turned into a wolf as he plunged into the water. Nine years later, since he had not tasted human flesh, he was free to come back and resume his former shape, which had aged during that time, as

if he had worn it all along. Another tale recounted how a man ate a child's entrails and was transformed into a wolf afterwards. In the *Satyricon*, a work of fiction dating from Ancient Rome, the courtier Petronius gave an account of a soldier who stripped naked, urinated, turned into a wolf, and ran away into the forest, howling. His companion picked up his clothes, which had turned to stone, and then went home to his mistress, only to find that the wolf had attacked her sheep in their fold.

....

MEDIEVAL HYSTERIA

Over the centuries, the wealth of European folklore surrounding the myth of the werewolf developed, in common with some other cultures, like that of the Native Americans. During the medieval period, when werewolf hysteria and paranoia about the supernatural was rife, the main features of the werewolf believed to be superhuman strength, extra-sensory perception, and great brutality. The werewolf was believed to enjoy eating recently deceased corpses, and was generally perceived as mad, destructive and evil.

However, there were those who claimed werewolves to be 'hounds of God'. One such was an old man named Theiss, who asserted that werewolves were faithful friends, just like real dogs, and that they descended to the depths of hell to do battle with demons, witches and evil spirits. Normally, in those days, he would have been burned at the stake for heresy, but because he was so old — aged 80 or so — the priests and judges thought his brain was addled, and sentenced him to 10 lashes of the whip instead.

....

EVIL EYE

The appearance of the werewolf also became more defined as the legend took shape. It was believed to be just like an ordinary wolf, only without a tail. It also had a human voice and human eyes. In human form, the werewolf was a person who seemed depressed and melancholic; indeed, in medieval times, mental illness was often explained by the notion that the sufferer was really a werewolf. In particular, psychiatric issues such as manic depression (also known as bipolar disorder), where the individual alternates between phases of energetic, elevated mood and deep despair, was seen as a distinct indicator that a person was, in secret, a werewolf.

There were many variations on the werewolf myth, according to different cultures and locations. In some accounts, werewolves were said to be transformed old women, or witches, who could paralyze children with their gaze. In others, such as in Serbian folklore, werewolves were said to strip off their skins, hang them on trees and return later to reclaim them.

....

SIGNS OF THE WOLF

There was a great deal of moralism attached to the werewolf cult in medieval times. It was claimed that there were evil people, such as witches and sorcerers, who were able, with their supernatural powers, to transform themselves into werewolves, so that they could commit brutal crimes. These kind of people were known as 'voluntary were-wolves'. Then there were innocent human beings, known as 'involuntary werewolves', who were born with tell-tale marks, such as having a lot of hair, curved fingernails and eyebrows that met in the middle. Such people might be unlucky enough to be born under a full moon, or to suffer from a disease like epilepsy. It was believed that they might be doomed by their lineage, being the seventh son of a seventh son was believed to carry the curse of the werewolf. In this case, in some cultures, the newborn baby with this heritage might be put to death. Sinners excommunicated by the church might also be punished, it was thought, by becoming werewolves.

....

MOON MAGIC

There were a number of ways in which werewolves could be identified, it was asserted. A person's flesh might be cut open to see if there was fur in the wound, or the tongue would be checked to see if there were bristles lying underneath it. There were also many different ways in which an individual might transform themselves into a werewolf. These might involve putting on a magic belt made of wolfskin, or rubbing a special lotion into the skin; drinking rainwater from a wolf footprint found in the forest; quaffing a potion brewed while reciting an incantation; or sleeping under a window so that the moon shone on the face.

The transformation was thought to be extremely painful, with bones cracking and skin being stretched as the body took on its new shape. According to the 16th-century antiquarian Richard Verstegan, human beings could transform themselves into werewolves by engaging in certain Satanic rituals. The medieval chronicler Gervase of Tilbury claimed that periods when there was a full moon enabled the transformation to take place. This idea, which was relatively uncommon at the time, later became a central part of werewolf lore, and was taken up by many modern fiction writers and film-makers.

····

SILVER BULLET

There were many beliefs about how to ward off, or kill, a werewolf. It was believed that werewolves dislike certain trees, such as the mountain ash, and could be kept at bay by plants such as rye grass, mistletoe, and wolfsbane (also known as aconite or Devil's Helmet). Unlike vampires, werewolves were thought to be impervious to such religious symbols as the Christian cross, or rituals such as the sprinkling of holy water. The notion that a werewolf could be killed by a silver bullet, or that an individual might become a werewolf after being bitten by a wolf, were later additions to the myth, and have come to play an important role in contemporary versions of the werewolf legend.

····

REMOVING THE CURSE

How can a person be cured of being a werewolf? Classical literature gives us several suggestions, including the idea that intense physical activity could exhaust the wolf, leading to the individual becoming a normal human being once again. In medieval times, the cures were, typically, rather more gruesome. They might have involved beating, piercing, or flaying the person's skin, sometimes leading to his or her death; incantations and religious rituals might have been used, including exorcism. If the individual was not a Christian, immediate conversion to Christianity might save the day; however, this was not always thought to be effective.

WEREWOLF ATTACKS

In France, during the 16th century, a massive panic about werewolves arose. The public became convinced that werewolf attacks were taking place all over the country, if not the world, and a number of suspects were identified. Among these were several members of the Gandillon family.

····

TORN LIMB FROM LIMB

Pernette Gandillon, a young woman suffering from the condition, ran about on all fours, imagining herself to be a wolf. When Pernette attacked a young lad of four years old, gashing his throat so that he bled to death, she was set upon by the local townspeople and torn limb from limb herself. Pernette's brother Pierre was also accused of being a werewolf, having, it was claimed, acquired a magic salve from the Devil, which caused him to turn into a shaggy wolf that attacked both animals and people. Pierre's son Georges and his daughter Antoinette also inherited this crazed behaviour, wreaking havoc on the community around them and causing several injuries and deaths in the process. The father, son and daughter were imprisoned, and according to witnesses, ran about howling in their cells, attacking anyone who came near them. Eventually, all three of them were hanged.

A GLOBAL CULT

The cult of the werewolf occurs in the folklore of many parts of the world. In Europe, there are stories of the French 'loup garou', the Spanish 'hombre lobo', the Slovenian 'volkodlak' and the Finnish 'ihmissusi', all forms of werewolves. In the Americas, we find 'skin walkers' and 'shape-shifters' among the Native American tribes, including the 'Mai-cob' of the Navajo people, and the 'nahual' of the Aztecs. It is believed that many of these figures and the legends surrounding them come from ancient Indo-European myths that have travelled the world with migrations of peoples from continent to continent, so that today, all the tales are distantly related to one another.

••••

MAN INTO WOLF

Some historians have put forward fascinating explanations as to how the werewolf legend was born. Robert Eisler published a book in 1948 called *Man Into Wolf*, which explains how, as humanity developed from hunter-gatherers to predators, individuals began to wear wolf skins and to take on the violent behaviour of wolves and other beasts of prey. In his view, the origins of the werewolf myths and legends found across the world are rooted in this history. Other scholars have pointed to the way that mental illness, rabies, porphyria, and several other medical conditions, were often explained by uneducated people in poor societies as having been caused by transformation into a werewolf. In early times, the behaviour of serial killers was also given a similar explanation, namely, that the killer had become a werewolf, losing all reason and humanity in the process.

••••••••••••••••••••••

A HORROR CHIEF

Today, the werewolf has become a staple of horror fiction, often pitted against the ever-popular vampire. The features of the modern-day werewolf have changed slightly from those of the past. There is more emphasis on the transformation taking place through a hereditary condition, or through the victim having been bitten by a wolf. There is also a focus on the pain and suffering caused by the transformation, by the body changing shape, the teeth becoming pointed and sharp claws tearing through nails. In addition, the wolf's amoral, cunning character is brought to the fore, as well as its superhuman strength. In some works of fiction, being cursed with the werewolf

alter ego is not necessarily a bad thing, as it brings out all the repressed confidence in the character, and in this sense, the protagonist is more free in his werewolf form than in his human one.

A 1905 illustration of the Romana tale *William of Palermo*. William is taken away by a werewolf.

A large number of novels and short stories about werewolves have been written from the 19th century to the present day, by famous authors such as Robert Louis Stevenson, Alexandre Dumas, J.R.R. Tolkein, Stephen King, Terry Pratchet and J.K. Rowling. Werewolves also feature in many horror films, TV series and popular computer games.

Section Three:

FOLKLORIC FREAKS

FOLKLORE CONSISTS OF stories which originated in particular communities, and the tales often feature characters which were once believed to exist. Usually, these characters have a sinister or mischievous edge, and would take immense pleasure in causing trouble for humans. Found in many tales of folklore are house spirits, sailor-tempting water sirens and man-made creatures. The house spirits are usually diminutive imps which live in a house, alongside a family with the domovoi, kobold, brownie and kikimora being different types of the house spirits. They behave differently, but are united in their ability to work harmoniously with humans, that is, unless they are angered or disrespected. The kikimora in particular can be a nasty housemate, and can use its powers to upset sleeping children, mercilessly tickling them or whistling repetitive tunes into their ears.

ASWANG

The aswang is a shape-shifting, bat-like demon from Filipino folklore. Since the 16th century it has been feared in the Western Visayan regions of the country, especially in the provinces of Capiz, Iloilo and Antique. It is always female, and is a hybrid creature combining the characteristics of a witch and a vampire. The aswang is an enormously powerful creature that, by day, assumes the form of an ordinary person and, by night, transforms into something hideously evil.

VULGAR POWERS

During the day the aswang is shy, quiet and elusive. Typically it will work somewhere connected to meat such as a butchers, because it craves being around flesh and guts. It will avoid attracting attention to itself in case anyone discovers its double life. By night the aswang sheds its human skin and transforms into a bat-like creature, stalking villages looking for dead bodies or young children to steal. It has vulgar powers, and often uses these in the most grotesque ways. One of these is using its proboscis to suck a foetus from the womb of a sleeping mother, to then feast on the tiny body. In other instances, it is said to be able to simply look at a pregnant woman and induce a miscarriage using its powers. If it steals a living child for sustenance, it will often leave a dummy baby behind, which will become ill and die. The aswang would often be blamed if miscarriages were suffered or if infants died.

....

GRAVE STALKER

The aswang is also partial to the recently deceased. It prowls around morgues and appears in disguise at wakes looking for dead bodies to steal. Strangely, the aswang will leave something in the place of the corpse, such as a banana trunk. The spell placed on the banana trunk allows it to pass off convincingly as a cadaver, but it will soon wear off leaving the grieving family to discover the truth, unless the body is buried quickly. If a human ever catches a glimpse into the aswangs eyes, it will notice how bloodshot they are, a result of staying up all night hunting. A human is unlikely to survive this encounter however, as the aswang has many powers, and can cause great pain and distress simply through eye contact. It has the ability to turn itself into other animals such as a pig, dog or bird, but has been most commonly sighted in the guise of a bat. At night, the aswang can be heard circling above houses, searching for a hole to enter through.

....

WARDING OFF AN ASWANG

In areas where aswangs are believed to live, there are several preventative measures employed by the local people. They believe the aswang is terrified of bullets, *bagakay* (sharpened bamboo spear), feathers and canes. Where possible, loaded guns are kept for defence purposes, bagakay and canes are stood in corners of rooms and piles of feathers are scattered sporadically on the floor. It is also believed that the aswang, much like the vampire, is repelled by garlic and crucifixes, and also can't stand to hear the name of God spoken. If confronted by an aswang, the repetition of the word 'God' may buy you a few seconds to get away while it stands there in horror.

....

KILLING AN ASWANG

The aswang moves quickly and silently, and if someone was to be brave enough to try and catch it, they would have real trouble even getting near it. However, if one is in a vulnerable position, a bagakay is an effective weapon against the aswang. If a bagakay is pierced into the creature's body, the aswang will become weak and be left with a wound that will not heal. It will then tear out the bagakay and scamper off, defeated. The next day, remembering the location of the wound, the brave one will then be able to identify the aswang in its human form, as the wound will still remain. It is when they are in their human state that the wound can be fatal, as the bagakay works like poison when it comes into contact with them, and only needs seconds to have an effect. One potential outcome of finding an injured human and declaring them the aswang is that in that moment, if they are not wounded badly enough, they may have enough strength left to transfer their powers onto a member of their family, who will then go on to avenge the aswang's death.

DOMOVOI

The Slavic 'domovoi' is a mischievous spirit that inhabits houses and lives alongside the family that reside there. It resembles an ugly old man, is small and completely covered in hair. The creatures vary in appearance. It may have a grey beard, or tails, or horns on its head, and in some cases it may resemble the former owner of the house. The domovoi is temperamental by nature. It can be caring and protective, but if it is crossed, it can be a most troublesome house guest.

THE TRICKSTER

The domovoi specializes in performing pranks; it must be respected, or it will cause havoc in the domestic sphere. According to tradition, a domovoi likes to be addressed as 'master', showing it respect. Some families will leave out a glass of milk or a plate of biscuits for their domovoi, to befriend it, so that it will become a protector and helper rather than a nuisance. The domovoi makes its home underneath the stove in the kitchen, or by the front door. For this reason, in Poland, when a new stove is put into a house, the owner first puts down a piece of bread for the domovoi. In Russia, a family moving house will put out an old boot for their domovoi to live in, so that he follows and helps them in their new abode. According to tradition, when moving house, the domovoi should be entreated to come too.

....

THE HOME HELP

As well as being a prankster, the domovoi can be persuaded to help with household chores and, if well cared for, can act as a guardian for the family. He may pull a woman's hair to warn her of danger, or start to howl or moan if danger is coming. On the other hand, the domovoi from a neighbouring household may cause endless trouble, harassing animals and stealing grain. If a domovoi is badly treated by its own family, it can be equally destructive, rattling or breaking crockery, banging pots, and leaving muddy footprints everywhere. At worst, if goaded, he may try to suffocate people in their beds, but this is uncommon.

....

THE KIKIMORA

Another Slavic house spirit is the 'kikimora', the female soul of an unbaptized child. She appears as a small, thin witch with long, untidy hair and a hunched back. According to some accounts, she wears dirty clothes, and has an ugly face. When angered, the kikimora is said to keep children awake at night, tickling them or whistling in their ears. At night, she is believed to come out and sit spinning in the kitchen. If any human being sees her at her work, they will die shortly afterwards.

....

THE RUSALKA

The 'rusalka' is a female, mermaid-like demon that lures men away from their wives and families. Slavic legend has it that she comes out of the water and sits singing songs in a tree, until she catches the attention of male workers in the fields. In some myths,

the rusalka is beautiful, with long hair and big green eyes, while in others, she is ugly and hirsute. She may take a man or child away by force, to live with her on the riverbed. Sometimes she can appear as a succubus (see page 29-31), with the purpose of tempting a man to have sex with her over and over again, until he became utterly exhausted. In this way she draws the life force out of him, and use it to sustain herself, in vengeance for a wrong that had been done to her in life.

The rusalka is a restless spirit who herself has died a violent death, perhaps committing suicide because of an unwanted pregnancy. If the young woman's death is avenged, her spirit is able to rest, and she will stop harassing the living. In other versions of the myth, the rusalka is thought of as an unbaptized, illegitimate child, whose mother has murdered it.

....

SCALES AND WEBBED FEET

The male counterpart of the rusalka is the 'vodyanoy', a river creature who looks like an ugly, naked old man with a long, unkempt beard. His body is covered in slimy black fish scales, and his hands are webbed, like a duck's feet. He has a tail like a fish, and burning red eyes. He rides about the river on a log, looking for people to drown, and when he succeeds, he drags them down to the bottom of the river to work for him as servants. When the captured victims die, he stores their souls in porcelain cups. Fishermen and millers were afraid of the vodyanoy, whom they considered to rule the river, and so they often made sacrifices to please him.

KOBOLD

In German mythology and folklore lives the kobold. The kobold is a house spirit or demon, the size of a small child, who lives among human beings in dwellings such as houses, ships and mines. Depending on the environment they inhabit, they have different manners and appearances; the kobold at sea dresses in finery and smokes pipes, the kobold in the peasant home dresses in rags and appears haggard. Their nature is similar to that of the domovoi; they must be respected or will wreak havoc.

GOBLINS AND TROLLS

Underground kobolds have much in common with goblins, the Scottish brownie, and the English boggart, all evil spirits that vex humankind. It's also been suggested that the cave-dwelling kobold, along with goblins and trolls, may have been modelled on the short-statured Northern peoples such as Finns and Lapps, who fled invasions of their countries and worked as blacksmiths in caves and mountains. These types of creatures are known to be small, ugly and prone to pranks and cruel tricks.

MORBID MANIFESTATIONS

The kobold appears to humans as a fiery flame, a point of light, or a small child. It can fly through the air, looking like a blue stripe, and may enter the house through a chimney. In the form of a child, it wears a red jacket and cap, but it can also become a wrinkled old man with red hair and a beard. In some variations of the myth, the kobold carries a knife, to remind the viewer that it was once a human being who was killed violently as a small child. The household kobold may be a beautiful boy with blond curly hair and a soft, tender voice; in contrast, the mine kobold is usually bent, twisted and grotesquely ugly, with soot ground into its skin.

ROAST ON A SPIT

Another common form that the kobold takes is an animal. This might be a bat, a snake or a worm, but it might also be a domestic animal such as a cat or a hen. Perhaps most disturbingly, the kobold may remain invisible, like a ghost, and then suddenly show itself in a terrifying way, sometimes as a naked man with a butcher's knife in his back, or as a dead baby floating in a cask of blood. Kobolds can be extremely brutal. In one legend, a kobold cuts a king into pieces, roasts him on a spit, and eats him. In another, a servant boy played a prank on the kobold, whereupon the kobold waited till he had gone to sleep, strangled him, tore his body limb from limb, and threw him into a boiling pot of water.

TRIO OF KOBOLDS

There are three types of kobolds. The household kobold may help with chores and, like the goblin, help a tradesman by working overnight at an extraordinary pace, to fulfil an order. However, if the kobold is mistreated or neglected it will play tricks on its master, and become a nuisance in the

The Kobold. Also known as
Robin Goodfellow or Puck.

household by breaking crockery, pulling out drawers and throwing objects about. If a family came into unexplained wealth, or a tradesman was very successful, the community around them would often suspect that their kobold had some hand in their good fortune.

····

SUBTERRANEAN KOBOLD

The kobolds that live in the mines appear somewhat disfigured, from years of hunching over to squeeze themselves into inaccessible areas of the caves. They work alongside the human miners, knocking to warn of danger, or indicating where precious metals might be found. It was thought that the kobold race were originally expert miners, toiling deep in the ground, side by side with their human counterparts. The kobold people, much like those that live above ground, do not take kindly to being disrespected, and would play tricks on the miners for revenge, sometimes fooling them into taking ore that, when smelted, proved to be worthless or even poisonous. Many mineworkers believed that the kobold actually lived within the rocks, just as human beings live in air.

····

KOBOLD AT SEA

The lore of Northern fishermen features a demon similar to the kobold called the 'klabautermann'. This creature helps the crew with all kinds of tasks such as repairing holes to the ship's hull, or pumping water out of the hold when the ship is in danger of sinking. It is thought to live in the wood of the ship, and may manifest itself as a ship's carpenter. However, if it is angered, it will tangle up ropes, mock the sailors and generally cause havoc on board. A common belief was that if the klabautermann made itself known, the person who saw it would die, and shortly afterwards, the ship would sink.

THE BOGEYMAN

Today, the word 'bogeyman' has come to signify a monster-like predator that hunts badly behaved children at night. He is used by parents as a tool to frighten their children into good behaviour. The child is told that the bogeyman lurks outside their bedroom, or hides in their closet or under the bed, and sometimes can suddenly materialize out of green fog. The bogeyman remains a very real threat in the imaginations of young people around the world.

BUGIS

The origin of the word 'bogeyman' is thought to lie in the southern part of Sulawesi, an island of Indonesia. The people there, known as Bugis, are mostly peaceful farmers, with a history of seafaring exploration, but in times gone by some of them were wild, brutal pirates who attacked the ships of English and Dutch traders. Thus, when European sailors brought back stories of the pirates, the name 'bugi man' came into being, meaning a violent marauder who may attack without warning. Some scholars disagree with this theory, claiming instead that the word 'bogeyman' links with many others in northern European languages, and was in use centuries before the era of English and Dutch colonization.

THE SACK MAN

In many cultures, especially Hispanic ones, the 'sack man', or 'hombre de la bolsa', as he is known, is said to be a nasty old man who puts children in his bag, carries them away, and then eats them. He is claimed to roam the streets at supper time, looking for disobedient children who stay playing outside when they have been called in. In some Hispanic cultures, instead of being called the 'sack man', he is known as 'el roba chicos' – the man who steals children.

BLACK PETE AND SANTA CLAUS

The 'sack man' has his counterpart in the 'bag man' of Armenia and Georgia; the 'torbalan' of Bulgaria; the 'mumus' of Hungary; the 'ocu' of Turkey; and the 'bubak' of the Czech Republic, Silesia and Poland. In many instances, he represents the opposite of the story of Father Christmas, who comes with his bag full of toys to give good children. In the Netherlands, the figure of 'Black Pete' is a servant of Santa Claus. Black Pete helps Santa deliver presents for Christmas, but he also rounds up bad children and takes them away to the North Pole in the empty toy bags. In some variants of the story, Black Pete was himself said to be a kidnapped child, taken by Santa Claus. As an adult, his job is to look for younger generations of servants who will replace him in his task when he grows old.

In some countries, the 'sack man' also takes adults away, hiding by riverbanks and making a crying noise like a baby, so that the adults will go searching for the infant. He is said to weave by moonlight, and his cart is drawn by a team of cats.

BABAU

In Italy and Romania, the menacing figure of 'Babau' has long been used to discipline children. Babau is said to be a tall man wearing a big black coat, with a black hood or hat covering his face. Traditionally, if a child will not eat its food, the parent will knock under the table and announce that Babau is at the door, waiting to take him or her away. A similar character, 'Butzemann', a man dressed in black with sharp claws and fangs, who abducts children that will not go to sleep, is found in Germanic cultures.

....

UNCLE GUNNYSACK

The bogeyman is also present in myths and legends of the West Indies, where he is sometimes dubbed 'Uncle Gunnysack', a giant who kidnaps naughty children. In Haitian Creole dialect, 'Uncle Gunnysack'

is known as Tonton Macoute; this was also the name given to the henchmen of the brutal dictator Papa Doc Duvalier, a secret police force made up of thugs and villains who visited political opponents in the night and took them away to prison, never to be seen again by their loved ones.

We also find the bogeyman in North India, as 'Bori Baba' ('Father Sack'); in Sri Lanka, as 'Goni Billa'; in Vietnam, as 'Ong Ba Bi' ('Mister Three Bags'); and in South Africa as 'Antjie Somers'. Somers is an escaped slave, a man who dresses up as a woman to disguise himself, and catches children in a bag, which he slings over his shoulder. A related myth is that of the Latin American 'El Cuco' or 'El Coco', a monster with a brown, hairy head like a coconut and glowing red eyes, who may have been a victim of violence himself but now seeks out children to kidnap.

BUNYIP

The bunyip, a 'water spirit', is part of Aboriginal lore. It is said to have a face like a dog, tusks like a walrus, a duck-like bill, a tail like a horse, large flippers and completely covered in black fur. In an 1878 publication entitled *The Aborigines of Victoria*, it is said to resemble an 'enormous starfish'. In another source, it is described as 11ft (3.3m) long, and very wide. Legend has it that the bunyip resides anywhere that is full of water: rivers, creeks, billabongs, waterholes and lakes.

THE CREATOR?

Descriptions of the appearance and nature of the bunyip varied greatly among the Aboriginal tribes in different parts of Australia — as did the name — as well as 'bunyip', the monster

was known as 'kianpraty'. Some scholars have linked the word 'bunyip' to 'bunjil', a god-like, great being in the form of a man, who had, according to Aboriginal mythology, made the heavens, the earth and all living creatures on it.

A carving of the bunyip existed at Fiery Creek, near Ararat, Victoria, in the late 19th century. According to the 19th-century antiquarian Reynell Johns, the carving, known as the Challicum Bunyip, had been made when the bunyip had been caught and speared after killing a man. Local Aboriginal people used to visit the spot every year, as a form of worship or penance.

····

ORIGIN OF THE BEAST

Whatever the truth, over the years many commentators have tried to explain the legend of the bunyip. Some say that the story arose when a seal was spotted in the river, having travelled up inland from the sea. According to Charles Fenner, a geologist and educator writing in the 1930s, this explained why the bunyip was said to be covered in fur, with bulging eyes, and a bellowing cry. Other experts, such as Dr George Bennett of the Australian Museum, and later, palaeontologist Pat Vickers-Rich, suggested that the bunyip might have become part of Aboriginal lore from prehistoric times, when the tribes may have encountered the bones of marsupials, or even the animals themselves, such as the Diprotodon, now extinct in Australia.

····

GIANT WOMBAT

The Diprotodon was an enormous beast the size of a hippopotamus, a plant-eating marsupial that would have weighed about three tonnes. Its existence was only discovered when large bones described as those of a 'giant wombat' were discovered on a farm in north-eastern Australia. The bones were put together to form the entire skeleton of a Diprotodon, the first of its kind ever to be completed. Another theory is that European settlers and explorers, who had never encountered Australian wild animals before, attributed some of their cries to the bunyip. For example, the Australasian bittern, a marsh-dwelling bird, emits a strange, low-pitched booming sound, which those unfamiliar with it might associate with a much larger animal. Today, for this reason, the bittern is sometimes known as 'the bunyip bird'.

····

SAVAGED BY A BUNYIP

The word 'bunyip', although it was long used by Aborigines, did not appear in print until 1845, when an article in a newspaper, *The Geelong Advertiser*, gave an account of fossil finds in the area. According to a local Aboriginal man, who had apparently been savaged by a bunyip, the creature had a head resembling an emu, with a long bill. The sides of the bill had razor-sharp, serrated edges. Its body was like that of an alligator, and it had thick, strong legs. The front legs were longer than those at the back, and the feet had long claws. In the water, the bunyip swam like a frog, while out on land it walked about on its hind legs, measuring up to 13ft (4m) high. According to the man, despite the bunyip's ability to tear its victim to shreds with its powerful beak and claws, it preferred to hug its prey to death.

····

ALLEGED SIGHTING

Another alleged sighting took place in 1852, when escaped convict William Buckley wrote an account of his years living with the Wathaurong tribespeople. He described seeing the monster, which he had learned about from them, swimming along one day in the river. He said it was approximately the size of a full-grown calf, with dusky grey feathers covering its body. However, he was unable to see its head or its tail.

Today, the bunyip has become part of contemporary culture, often cited in children's literature, and appearing in role play and computer games such as *RuneScape* and *AdventureQuest*.

Medieval monsters of land, sea and air from *Puch der Natur*. Hand coloured woodcut reproduction of a medieval German illustration printed in Augsburg 1478.

The Golem: How He Came into the World. Poster for the 1920 silent horror masterpiece starring Paul Wegener.

GOLEM

The golem is a creature of Jewish folklore, a monster created out of unformed matter. In some respects, he is rather like Frankenstein's monster, often seen as a kind of brainless hulk, servant to a much more intelligent person. Over the centuries, the word 'golem' has changed, in Yiddish, to 'goylem', meaning a person who is slow-witted and clumsy.

MUD OF CREATION

According to early Jewish scripture, the golem was originally formed by God, or a higher being, or a holy person (such as a rabbi), out of clay, mud or dust. In the Hebrew bible, the first man, Adam, was himself created as a golem. The bible told the story of how God kneaded the mud of creation into a roughly formed being, without giving it — at first — the power to speak. Later, the golem was given the gift of some holy words, inscribed on its forehead, which enabled it to move about and talk. It was believed that, if the inscription was taken away, the golem returned once more to being a lifeless hulk.

This power to take away the golem's ability to act was very important. Certain learned rabbis were said to be able to control the golem, who otherwise would have grown to an enormous size, it was believed, and would have destroyed the entire world. The monster was thought to be extremely violent when roused, killing non-Jewish people, and spreading alarm and panic. The way the rabbis controlled the golem was to remove the holy inscription on the golem's forehead, whereupon it would disintegrate, so that it no longer posed a threat to civilized society.

....

THE RABBI'S GOLEM

In the 16th century, the Chief Rabbi of Prague, Judah Loew ben Bezalel, created a golem in order to stop the Prague ghetto being attacked by anti-Semitic hordes. The golem was fashioned out of the clay of the Vltava — river that runs through the city — and animated through sacred rituals and chanting. Unfortunately, the golem grew too large, and began to run about killing the gentiles it encountered. Because of this, the rabbi rubbed out the word inscribed on the golem's forehead, and it fell down dead. Its body was taken to the synagogue and placed in the attic, where, according to legend, it still lies. Should the Jews be attacked again, the golem can, according to legend, be brought to life.

Later, historians rejected the truth of the story, not least because, when the attic of the synagogue in question was renovated, there proved to be no trace of the alleged golem. However, the legend has remained a central one in Czech culture, also inspiring writers, artists and film-makers around the world.

....

THE TROUBLE WITH GOLEM

The idea of the golem is a complex one. On the one hand, the golem is a being that, because of its great strength and size, may be able to protect a community. On the other, the golem is known to be stupid, so it may be unable to interpret instructions intelligently, and may carry out violent attacks as a result of misunderstanding or, simply due to its hostile nature. In this respect, the golem of Jewish folklore resembles such monsters as the zombie from Haitian folk tales: strong, servile, but ultimately without the intelligence or humanity to be merciful. However, in a similar way to the Frankenstein myth, and the legend of King Kong, some writers have created stories in which the golem does experience human emotions, such as falling in love, only to be disappointed and angered when it is rejected by the object of its affections.

The golem myth has been periodically updated by writers and film-makers from different cultures. In the early 20th century, Gustave Meyrink's novel *The Golem* was inspired by the mindless creature, as was Paul Wegener's classic film, *The Golem: How He Came into the World*, released in 1920. In the 1960s, the legend of the golem formed the basis of the film *It!*, released in 1966, while in 1974, the character of the golem was introduced into Marvel Comics' *Strange Tales* series. Golems have also appeared in the novels of Pete Hamill, Michael Chabon, Terry Pratchett, David Brin and Marge Piercy. The golem monster also features in some episodes of the TV series *The X Files*, and is a popular character in games such as Dungeons and Dragons.

The Golem of Prague, Old Town Square, Prague, Czech Republic.

TROLLS

A troll is a member of a mythical anthropomorphic race from Scandinavian folklore. They are sometimes thought of as fiendish giants akin to ogres, and in other parts of the world they are seen as sneaky, diminutive tricksters that lurk in the woods. Some say they are simple-minded, some say they are highly-intelligent, but all can agree that they are frightfully ugly.

MONSTROUS BRUTES

There are two main traditions in the Scandinavian folklore of trolls. In some areas, they are thought of as large, idiotic, solitary creatures who dwell in caves or mountains. They are portrayed as being exceptionally ugly, with wrinkled skin and a single, bulging eye positioned above a fat, hideous nose. These trolls, like ogres, are stupid and can be commanded to carry out tasks which utilize their enormous size and strength. In other portrayals they are manipulative and use their cunning to trick others. They spend their days hiding away in mountains, and their nights trawling the woods for human meat, holding their clubs up high, ready to bring down on their victim's head. When the 1841 Norwegian fairy tale *Billy Goats' Gruff* became known worldwide, it was this representation of the fearsome troll living under

A Norwegian troll by Reginald Knowles, 1910.

the bridge which, firstly, brought trolls to prominence, and secondly, established a firm perception of the character of a troll.

····

SHAPE-SHIFTING TRICKSTERS

The second tradition portrays trolls as creatures that live in the woods, either inside concealed caves or in an underground lair, accessible via a strategically-placed boulder. According to some sources they are as short as dwarves, in others they are human-sized. In comparison to the destructive, brutish larger trolls, these are greedy, selfish and sneaky creatures with special powers. They are great shape-shifters, and can transform into a variety of objects or sizes, including animals such as cats or dogs. Legend has it that female trolls are identifiable in their human guise, as they dress elegantly, and hunters would find this suspicious if they encountered them in the woods. Often a hunter that crossed the path of a female troll would find himself under her spell, and sometimes he would be trapped as her companion, slave or pet. Decades later, when the troll tired of him and released him, he would find his way home again, with no recollection of his missing years. Women and children were at risk of abduction too, and the trolls would occasionally steal a newborn baby and leave their own offspring in its place.

····

THEFT AND SABOTAGE

Another power held by these smaller trolls is the ability to turn themselves invisible. This particular capability made their hobby of stealing easy to pursue, and they would turn invisible and enter into houses undetected. Mischievous by nature, they would revel in the opportunity to cause havoc and not be caught, and would often steal food directly off a plate and throw crockery across the room as the humans gasped in horror. They also enjoyed teasing farmers, and would sabotage crops or hide equipment, anything to make life difficult.

····

TURNED TO STONE

There are not many known methods of warding off a troll. Similar to the vampire myth, it is believed that they do not like to hear the name of Christ, and repeatedly chanting this word in their presence would send them running. It is thought that trolls cannot tolerate being exposed to sunlight, and that as soon as the sun comes up they turn to stone. Legend has it that the presence of misshapen rocks or random boulders would be assumed to be the remains of a troll, one who had been surprised by the rising sun and paid the price.

····

GOOD LUCK CHARM

Today, the figure of the troll has evolved from the gigantic dim-witted creature of folklore, and become a character employed in many other mediums. In the 1960s a troll doll was produced by a Danish woodcutter, as a gift for his young daughter. It had sheep wool hair and glass eyes, and when the little girl showed her friends, they all wanted one too, and he soon began producing them to order. Eventually the idea got picked up by manufacturers (including Hasbro and Mattel) overseas, and their popularity continued to soar for the next three decades, making these troll dolls collectible items. From this one idea also came a spin-off television show and talks of a feature film. Taking the character of a troll and reproducing it in a positive way has reinvented the myth to a certain degree, and these particular toys are now seen as good luck charms, a million miles away from the child-eating troll of Scandinavian lore.

Troll Hunter

— 2010 —

Scene from 2010 Norwegian movie *Trolljegeren* (*The Troll Hunter*). Three students investigate a series of mysterious bear killings, but soon discover that it isn't bears doing the killings but giant killer trolls. They follow a mysterious hunter who works for a secret government agency. Several dangerous trolls have escaped from their reservations and the hunter has been assigned to eliminate them.

GOBLIN

Goblins are mischievous creatures which feature, in some form, in various folklore around the world. They can be the size of an adult human, or as tiny as a fairy. They are usually hideously ugly, with crooked teeth and large noses. They are playful and naughty by nature, and like to mock human expressions by twisting their faces into grotesque grimaces.

BLOOD-CURDLING SMILE

The goblins of English folklore grow up to 30 cm (12 in) in height and are absolutely grotesque to look at. Their brow, along with the rest of their body, is covered with thick, dark hair. Their mouth is crammed full with yellow, crooked teeth which seem to fester with some otherworldly disease. Like the trow (see below) they are said to be invisible to most people, although a special few have the ability to see them. It is said that a goblin's smile curdles blood and its laugh has the power to sour milk, because of this, the presence of a goblin was often blamed if milk had gone off overnight. Some claim they are stupid creatures, others say they are fiendish and cunning. They are sarcastic and rude, and often like to contort their faces into grimaces, mocking human expressions. They are pranksters by nature and love nothing more than to wreak havoc on humans, usually entering their homes at night, and moving furniture about. They like to bang pots and pans together in the kitchen, knock on windows and open doors just to slam them shut. On farms, goblins were said to steal horses and ride them all night long. If a horse was tired in the morning, the farmer would know a goblin had been there, and if a horse was panicking, he'd know a goblin was, at that moment, trying to mount it.

THE BROWNIE

Goblins have connections to the brownie of Scottish and English folklore. The brownie is a cross between a goblin and a fairy, and is thought of as a 'household spirit'. At one time, it was believed that every household had its own brownie. In English folklore, the brownie lived in an unused part of the house, and in Scottish folklore, it lived in streams or any other water source it could find outside. The brownie is more hard-working than a standard goblin, and performs a series of tasks within a house in exchange for food and water. It does not like to be seen by humans and will only undertake these jobs at night.

TROWS OF ORKNEY

In the ancient mounds scattered across the Orkney Islands lives a race of ugly, deformed, stunted creatures known as trows. They are considerably smaller than adult humans, always walk backwards and are hideously ugly. It is believed that they are nocturnal as they are rarely seen during the day. Trows have the power to turn themselves invisible, and legend has it that only certain people are blessed with the ability to see them in this state. This ability, however, can be shared to one who does not possess it, simply by touching hands. It was believed that trows, much like other varieties of goblins, would visit houses at night. They would go in and sit by the fire, and the horrified residents would lie in bed listening to their invisible intruders moving around downstairs. They live in earthen-mound dwellings known as 'trowie knowes', which are, according to legend, filled with only the finest food and drink and covered in gold and silver.

· · · ·

LOVERS OF MUSIC

They have an insatiable passion for music, and many folk tales are still told to this day of trows luring fiddlers down into their homes, and commanding they play music for them. The fiddler would emerge from the earth days later, convinced he had only been down there for one day. One famous story in trow lore involves a particularly successful fiddler, who pleased the trows so much that they said he would never be short of money. From that day onwards, whenever he needed money he would simply put his hand in his pocket and pull out shining gold coins. One day, when this lucky man was drunk on home-brewed beer, he let slip to his friend about his 'trowie shilling'. This confession broke the spell and from that moment he never had another trowie shilling to spend.

A 17th century witchcraft scene with goblins dancing in the foreground.

ONI

The Oni are fearsome demons in Japanese folklore. They have a humanoid form, but hideous features which fill it. They have wild hair, two devil-like horns protruding from their foreheads, sharp claws and numerous eyes, toes and fingers. They fly, with formless arms outstretched, hunting for the souls of those who were evil in their mortal lives.

DISASTER BRINGERS

Oni were originally believed to be invisible spirits which were responsible for bringing disaster and disease into the world. When Buddhism was introduced into Japan, features of that faith were blended into Japanese mythology, and the result was that the oni took on more human attributes, and became thought of as a demonic ogre-like figure, instead of a wispy ghost. Oni was often used, and still is to this day, as a tool to encourage good behaviour in children, much like the Bogeyman myth in the West. Despite the belief that oni were primarily interested in searching for damaged souls to steal, parents would tell their children that the oni would come and get them if they did not behave. There is an expression, 'oya ni ninu ko wa oni no ko', which literally translates to, 'a child that does not resemble its parents is the child of an oni'. Depending on how it was used, this phrase could be taken to mean that a child who does not behave in the way instructed by its parents must be the spawn of the worst being imaginable. In its more literal sense the expression implies that if a child does not physically take after its biological parents then it must be an offspring of the dreaded oni. Japanese children are brought up with the concept of the oni as a fearsome figure to such an extent that when playing the game 'tag', the player who is 'it', is instead the oni.

SETSUBUN FESTIVAL

In Japan, the Setsubun Festival (Bean-Throwing Festival) is held annually on 3 or 4 February, the day before the beginning of spring, and in accordance with the lunar new year. The purpose of the festival is to cleanse away the evil spirits from the year that had just passed, and drive away any which are coming in the new year. It is believed that malevolent spooks would choose the start of a new year to enter the mortal realm, and by performing the special ritual it helps keep them at bay. Chasing away demons is achieved by roasting soybeans and throwing them around the home, at temples and at shrines. While scattering the soybeans, the following words should be shouted, 'Oni wa soto! Fuku wa uchi!', which means, 'Devils out, happiness in!'. Then, the number of soybeans which correspond to the soybean-throwers age should be picked up, and eaten. In addition to the roasted soybeans, it is common practice to hang holly around a house in order to keep the oni away, and to display statues or ornaments of monkeys.

WENDIGO

The Wendigo is a cannibalistic monster which features in the mythology of Algonquian-speaking people, that is, the native people from sporadic locations in North America and Canada. The wendigo was known to come out at night and hunt for human flesh in the woods. They were a greatly feared creature, because as well as their ability to tear a human to pieces, they were also capable of possessing a man, and transforming him from person to beast.

SKELETAL CORPSE

The wendigo has been described as a cross between a werewolf, Bigfoot and a troll. This combination illustrates its flesh-hungry, but there are aspects of its appearance which are more like that of a zombie. It has a skeletal body, with bones protruding from its grey, corpse-like skin. Its eyes are sunk deep into their sockets, and its dry and shrivelled lips are stained with blood. Inside its mouth is a putrid tongue covered in slime, and pointed yellow fangs emerge from its rotten gums. The monster emits such a stomach-churning odour that it was believed a wendigo could be smelt, before it could be seen.

Wendigos are enormously tall and paper thin; so thin, in fact, that if they stood to the side they would not be visible. They have an insatiable appetite for human flesh, one which can never be satisfied. They roam the woods at night looking for victims, and when they select one and devour it, their body grows in proportion to the human it had just consumed. The relief from eating lasts a second or two, and then the unbearable hunger returns. The wendigo's appetite gets more intense after every meal, and the constant eating and subsequent growing leads the monster to quickly be ravenous again, but always appear emaciated.

BECOMING A WENDIGO

Legend has it that there are several ways a person may become a wendigo. Firstly, if they eat human flesh it is thought that this triggers a transformation into the beast. However, sceptics have speculated that this myth was invented to discourage tribe members from descending into cannibalism in times of famine. The fear of becoming a wendigo through cannibalism was so intense that suicide was considered a preferable option amongst tribespeople. It was also believed that being bitten by a wendigo may infect the victim with a craving for human flesh, leading to the victim eventually transforming into the monster. There is no reversal process for this, and so tribe members were very nervous of getting bitten. According to some sources, wendigos were seen as embodiments of gluttony and greed, and those who embraced a life of excess were at a huge risk of becoming a wendigo as punishment. The threat of this is said to have taught many the importance of moderation, but it is claimed that some could not shake their selfish addictions, and were transformed into a wendigo as a result. There is believed to be only one way to kill a wendigo: burning it alive and then scattering the ashes.

····

WENDIGO PSYCHOSIS

A culture-bound syndrome, or folk illness, is a disorder which affects a particular group or community. In the communities of the Algonquian people, a disorder existed called Wendigo Psychosis. This involved sufferers developing an unquenchable desire to eat human flesh, even at times when food supplies were plentiful. Individuals inflicted with the disorder believed they were turning into a wendigo and would request to be executed. Attempts to treat them using traditional native healing remedies or Western doctors were largely successful, but if treatment failed they would execute the sufferer. There is little documented proof that this happened, but there is one famous story of a man afflicted with the condition.

····

SWIFT RUNNER

In the harsh winter of 1878, a Cree (Algonquian language native to Canada) man named Swift Runner and his family were starving. When his eldest son perished, he began to feel the influence of the wendigo spirit overcome him. He took an axe, and turned it on his wife and remaining five children, savagely butchering them for their flesh. He consumed every last inch of their bodies, and when the authorities found out they quickly arrested him. There was then a debate over whether Swift Runner was a 'true' cannibal or not. The distance from Swift Runner's house to the local food supply store, Hudson's Bay Company, was 25 miles, and it was this which proved he did not kill his family for sustenance, but because he was affected by Wendigo Psychosis. He was

hung regardless, and became the first legally executed man in Alberta, Canada in 1879.

····

JACK AND JOSEPH FIDDLER

Jack Fiddler, also known as Zhauwuno-geezhigo-gaubow, was an Oji-Cree chief and shaman. He claimed he could use his powers to defeat wendigos, and cure people that were afflicted with Wendigo Psychosis. Jack worked with his brother, Joseph, and one of their methods of helping sufferers was to euthanize them. In 1907 the authorities caught up with the Fiddler brothers, and they were arrested for the murder of 14 people. Jack managed to escape from custody while being taken on a supervised walk outside the prison grounds — several hours later the police found his body hanging from a tree. Meanwhile, Joseph was sentenced to life imprisonment for his crimes. After a series of appeals from his family, and taking into account the good intentions that Joseph claimed were behind the euthanized patients, he was granted a pardon in 1909. He died in jail three days before he was due to receive the news.

····

HISTORICAL PHENOMENON

Reports of Wendigo Psychosis cases ceased in the 20th century, as the native Algonquian people began to be influenced by Western ideologies. Over the years there have been debates over the authenticity of Wendigo Psychosis as a genuine disorder. Some have speculated that the theory behind the syndrome is simply the product of the misinterpreted wendigo myth. However, there are a number of credible accounts of the disorder that indicate that Wendigo Psychosis is, in reality, a historical phenomenon.

BABA YAGA

Baba Yaga is a witch-like character who roams the forest hunting for children to kidnap and eat. She lives in a hut which moves about on yellow chicken legs. She is a famous character in the world of fairy tales and folklore, and appears in many Russian and Eastern European stories.

. . . .

THE RUSSIAN WITCH

The story of Baba Yaga has been told for generation in Russian folklore, and was presumably a character invented to frighten children into behaving. She's a haggard old witch that is believed to be the Devil's own grandmother. There are numerous versions of the Baba Yaga story, but generally all versions agree on her hideous appearance and her unusual home. Baba Yaga is grotesque to look at, with her mouth crammed with iron teeth and her nose which is so long it touches the ceiling of the hut she lives in. She has wrinkled skin and long, greasy hair which flows from her head and chin, making her look extremely wild when she flies through the night sky. She travels around the woods inside a large mortar, and, holding the gigantic pestle in her right hand, she pushes herself along. She is so tall and thin that when she sits in the mortar her knees touch her chin. In her left hand she holds a broom made of silver birch, and she uses this to sweep away the path behind her, removing any trace that she was ever there.

CHICKEN LEGS

Baba Yaga lives in a hut deep in the forest. The hut sits upon two tall, skinny, bright yellow chicken legs and moves about the forest, spinning rapidly as it goes. A blood-curdling screech can be heard as the hut roams around the woods, and it will only stop when a special incantation is uttered. When it hears the magical phrase and comes to a halt, it will slowly lower its chicken legs down and throw its doors open with a crash that is so loud it shakes all the trees in the forest. When the hut is at 'home', it is surrounded by a fence made of bones, and at the top of each post sits a skull with glowing eyes. If a visitor comes across the hut and wants to enter, Baba Yaga appears and asks if they have come of their own free will or if they were sent. If anyone was ever daft enough to go in, they would certainly not be coming out again. Inside her hut, she sleeps on top of a giant oven. Her body is so long that her limbs touch the walls, her nose touches the ceiling and her hair spills out the windows. She keeps a large spatula in the hut, and uses it to push the bodies of children into the oven. Baba Yaga has a huge appetite, and can eat enough human flesh in one sitting to feed 10 men.

Depiction of Baba Yaga with her broom, Vassilla the
Beautiful. J. A. Billibine circa 1900.

THE LAMBTON WORM

Around the River Wear, County Durham, England, there is a famous piece of folklore which is still told to this day. A mysterious creature was plucked from the river, and over the years transformed into a terrifying creature. In some variations of the myth it is a dragon, in others it is a serpent; but in the beginning, it was only a tiny little worm.

CATCH OF THE DAY

John Lambton was born into a noble family, and became heir to the Lambton Estate, which included a Castle in which was the impressive Grand Hall. One Sunday, when everyone else in the village was at mass at Brugeford Chapel, John went fishing in the River Wear. He felt guilty about missing mass, and wondered if he was being punished for not attending, as he didn't catch a single fish for hours. He cursed the river for not offering him a decent fish to take home, and then suddenly he felt something on his hook. He could feel that it had enormous strength and assumed it must be absolutely huge. He struggled for a long time to pull it out of the water, but when he saw it he was shocked at how tiny it was. It was completely black, had the appearance of a worm but with the head of a salamander, and rows of razor sharp teeth. It had nine holes along each side of its mouth, and it secreted a slime as it wriggled on the bank. Though it was a minute little creature, it seemed to wriggle with immense power. As he stared at the mini-beast and wondered what to do with it, an old man appeared from nowhere. 'It bodes no good for you but you must not cast it back into the river, you must keep it and do with it what you will.' The old man disappeared as quickly as he had arrived,

and John felt the whole encounter had been extremely eerie. He put the creature in his catch basket and started walking home to Lambton Castle. Suddenly he could hear the old man's voice in his head again, and the words played over and over. As he stared at his hideous catch, a feeling of unease and terror washed over him. He threw it into an ancient well near the Great Hall and carried on back to the castle.

EVIL LURKING IN THE DEPTHS

Several years went by and John was called away to fight in the crusades. Little did he know that back home, the forgotten worm was still at the bottom of the well. He could not have imagined in his wildest dreams that over the years it had grown into a fearsome serpent, and become even more powerful with each passing day. The water in the well became undrinkable, and any who tasted it would be stricken down from the poisonous effects. The villagers knew that something strange was happening, and they traced the problem back to the well. They speculated that the well was cursed, and that something evil must be lurking in the depths. However, one morning, the speculation ended. The villagers awoke to discover a serpent in the river, wrapped three times around a rocky island. A trail of black slime linked the well

THE LAMBTON WORM

to the river, and they knew that it was the beast that had caused the well to become poisonous. People came from far and wide to catch a glimpse of the monster, who mostly sat at the rock during the day and coiled itself around a hill during the night, leaving spiral imprints in the grass. The monster's body rippled as it moved, and its razor sharp teeth that John had noticed when he originally caught the beast were longer, and sharper than before. The poisonous vapours which had been seen coming out of the well could now be seen pouring out of its nostrils and mouth, like thick plumes of smoke.

CHANGE OF MOOD

The monster's good nature was not to last, however. It soon became hungry, and with its ultra-sensitive sense of smell it could detect milk from miles away. It stopped sitting by the river, and started venturing onto land, hunting for sheep and cows to tear apart and eat. In some variations of the story, children were also his prey, and if a child happened to go missing in the village, the beast would be blamed. The locals became braver in response to the monster's escalating violence, and started attacking it. But it was stronger than them, and many found themselves with the monster's tail wrapped round them, held under the water until they drowned. Others met their end in its jaws, pierced by its rows of teeth, each like a giant kitchen knife.

The Lambton Worm, from Churchman's cigarette cards *Legends of Britain* series 1936.

A HAPPY ARRANGEMENT

One day, the monster was spotted heading in the direction of Lambton Castle. The villagers gathered in the Great Hall and devised a plan. They gathered as much milk together as possible, and filled a large stone trough. As the beast approached, it became distracted by the scent of the milk, and buried its head in the trough, drinking back as much as it could. Once its appetite was satisfied, it slivered back to the river, and disappeared into the depths. This occasion started a tradition that would endure for seven years. The monster left the animals on the hills alone, and the locals stopped trying to kill it. It would go up to the gates of the Great Hall and be given an offering of milk, and in return it would not bother the community. A few times during these seven years, there were several attempts to slay the monster, but each failed, with the warriors meeting the same fate as those that tried in the beginning.

....

RETURN OF JOHN

John Lambton returned to his village, victorious from battle and now a bona fide Sir. He was soon informed of what had happened in his absence, and knew it was up to him to rid the village of the monster once and for all. He went to see a witch that lived in Brugeford, and she told him, 'You and you alone can kill the worm, go to the blacksmith, and have a suit of armour wrought with razor sharp spear heads studded throughout its surface. Then go to the worm's rock and await its arrival. But mark my words well, if you slay the beast you must put to death the first thing that crosses your path as you pass the threshold of Lambton Hall. If you do not do this then three times three generations of Lambtons will not die in their beds.' Sir John swore an oath to do as the witch advised, and went straight to the blacksmith to have his armour fashioned.

....

THE BATTLE

The next day, Sir John put on his specially-made armour, and headed to the river to fight the monster. It emerged from the water, and battle commenced. Every time the beast tried to wrap its body around its opponent, pieces of its flesh were torn off by the spikes on Sir John's armour. After some time, the worm-turned-monster began to tire, and all that was needed was one final hit of the sword to finish it. Sir John brought his sword down hard on the monster's neck, slicing his head clean off. He triumphantly let out three blasts on his bugle, signalling his success to the villagers, and commanding that his servant should release one of his hounds so he could complete the oath. Unfortunately, amid the commotion, his father came upon Sir John before the hound could. He could not bring himself to kill his own father, and so the witch's prophesy was fulfilled, and for nine generations no Lambton died in their bed. The curse came true, at least for the first three generations of Lambton men after Sir John passed away.

....

PENSHAW MONUMENT

Today, a construction based on an Ancient Greek temple sits on top of Penshaw Hill, on land which formerly belonged to the Lambton Estate. It is called the Penshaw Monument and is dedicated to the memory of the first Earl of Durham. It is believed to be the final resting place of the worm. Spiral patterns can still be seen in the earth, and are believed to have been caused by the monster, as it coiled itself around the hill three times all those years ago.

Section Four:
REVILED REVENANTS

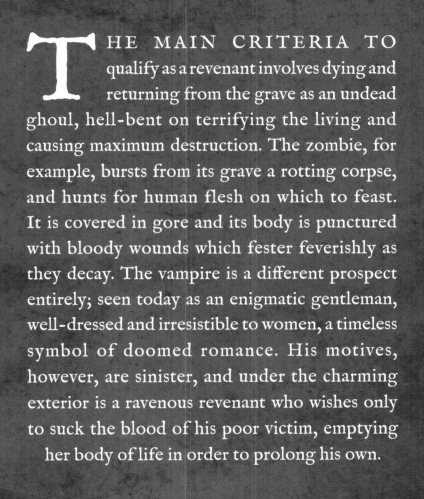

THE MAIN CRITERIA TO qualify as a revenant involves dying and returning from the grave as an undead ghoul, hell-bent on terrifying the living and causing maximum destruction. The zombie, for example, bursts from its grave a rotting corpse, and hunts for human flesh on which to feast. It is covered in gore and its body is punctured with bloody wounds which fester feverishly as they decay. The vampire is a different prospect entirely; seen today as an enigmatic gentleman, well-dressed and irresistible to women, a timeless symbol of doomed romance. His motives, however, are sinister, and under the charming exterior is a ravenous revenant who wishes only to suck the blood of his poor victim, emptying her body of life in order to prolong his own.

ZOMBIE

Second only to the vampire in popularity, the zombie is one of the most enduring of modern monsters. At first sight, it may seem difficult to see why: in contrast to the dark charm of the vampire, the zombie is a hideous, stupid, shuffling creature, a rotting corpse with severed limbs, covered in blood and gore, with a taste for live human flesh. Yet it has become a staple of the horror genre, exploring some of the most disturbing aspects of modern life, whether from a horrific or comical perspective.

THE VOODOO ZOMBIE

The original zombie comes from the ancient folklore of Haiti, in particular from aspects of the Vodun or Voodoo religion. The religion came initially from Africa, brought to the West Indies by slaves. It was banned by slave masters, but survived in a new, disguised form, with elements of Roman Catholicism added to it, as well as remnants of Amerindian belief systems. Over the years, it developed a reputation as a sinister form of witchcraft practised by black people, especially among the slaves of Haiti. In particular, stories of sorcerers raising individuals from the dead as zombies, of voodoo dolls, of human sacrifices, and so on, were rife, although these were often exaggerated.

····

CHARMS AND SPELLS

Haitian voodoo followers believed in the power of sorcerers known as *houngan* (a priest) or *mambo* (a priestess), who were said to be able to raise the dead, through magic spells and rituals. Over the years, as the economic situation of Haiti fell into decline, the commercial aspect of voodoo was emphasized with the sorcerer (now known as *bokor*) prac-

tising the black arts and selling charms and spells, or *ouangas*, for money. Certain rituals of folklore, such as the practice of nailing small wooden dolls to a tree near a cemetery, in the belief that the dolls would be able to carry messages from the dead, were given a new, sinister twist, with the sorcerer claiming to be able to bring misfortune on a victim by sticking pins into a small effigy.

····

STEALING THE SOUL

In the Voodoo religion, the soul is composed of two parts, the *gro bonanj*, and the *ti bonanj*. The former migrates after death, while the latter, which represents the person's will, remains. It is this part that, according to lore, the bokor is able to steal away from a live human being, capturing it so that the person is left with no personality or will. Once the will is captured, the bokor can force the person to work for him as a slave, labouring ceaselessly without the power, or indeed the desire, to change the situation.

Clearly, this legend acted as a powerful symbol of the history of Haiti, a place where throughout the centuries, both the people — and the land — itself have been ruthlessly exploited by a series of greedy rulers, whether European colonists or the black elite, such as the tyrant Papa Doc Duvalier and his son Baby Doc. The blank-eyed zombie who has lost the will to rebel, living a miserable life and forced to endure a life of hard labour as a slave until he or she finally drops dead from exhaustion, has for hundreds of years, been a tragic reality in the country.

· · · ·

NIGHTMARE HISTORY

Even today, Haiti remains the poorest nation in the Western hemisphere, with 80 per cent of the population living below the poverty line. Little wonder that, in the earthquake of January 2010, the country suffered such devastation; badly built housing, minimal emergency services and deforested countryside were all to blame. Strangely, the people emerging from the ruined towns and cities, dazed and covered in white dust, were reminiscent of the zombies of legend, reminding us that zombie lore is in many ways, an expression of the reality of life in a culture with a nightmare history.

· ·

ZOMBIE CREATION

According to tradition, there are several methods that the sorcerer, or *bokor*, uses to create a zombie. Firstly, he may use a potion to drug the live individual, causing the victim to enter into a trance-like state. This potion may contain a poison extracted from the pufferfish, which induces numbness, dizziness and vomiting. Paralysis of the entire body ensues, and the victim seems to stop breathing. The victim may lapse into a coma for several days, during which time he or she will be conscious, but unable to move or speak.

· · · ·

BURIED ALIVE

The potion may also contain animal parts, including blood and hair. It may be admin-

istered as a powder, brewed as a drink, or injected by blow dart, known as the 'coup padre'. When victims become comatose, they may be presumed dead and taken to the graveyard to be buried. Of course, if they are still conscious while all this is happening, the experience is horrific.

· · · ·

REANIMATED CORPSE

Legend has it that, once the body is buried, the *bokor* secretly goes to the graveyard at night, exhumes the corpse and performs a variety of rituals over it. The aim is to trap the *ti bonanj*, or soul, in a small clay jar, which is then wrapped up with some of the victim's possessions, such as jewellery or a fragment of clothing. The victim now has no soul or will, and in this way, the reanimated corpse becomes the slave of the *bokor*, destined to serve his master until his death.

Carrying on the zombie fascination; a scene from *Dylan Dog: Dead of Night* (2011)

A crawling zombie from the TV series
The Walking Dead in which police officer
Rick Grimes leads a group of survivors
in a world overrun by zombies.

In the next step of the reanimation process, the victim is given a dose of the datura plant, known in Haiti as the 'zombie's cucumber'. This plant, also known as Angel's Trumpet and Hell's Bells, contains toxic hallucinogens and was even used to treat various respiratory conditions before being banned for medical purposes. Strangely, those under the influence of it may have completely unreal but ordinary experiences, such as drinking a cup of tea, but completely lose the ability to distinguish between what is real and what is imaginary.

···

REAL ZOMBIES?

There are many theories regarding the truth behind the zombie myth. Some believe that the legend has some basis in reality, in that sorcerers in Haiti used powerful hallucinogenic drugs as part of their rituals and ceremonies. Others point to the history of Haiti, especially the period of the Tontons Macoutes, soldiers of the Duvalier regime named after the bogeymen of Haitian folklore, who were so brutal — and loyal to their tyrannical leader — that the people believed them to be zombies who had completely lost their humanity and their free will.

···

THE TRUTH EMERGES

The case of Felicia Felix-Mentor, a woman who had apparently died and was buried in 1907, but reappeared in 1936, half-naked and confused, led many to believe a real zombie was walking the streets. According to a Haitian professor of psychiatry, Louis P. Mars, the woman was simply mentally ill, and had been mistaken for the dead woman; however, it was agreed the two women were spookily alike. Mars also commented on the research of folklorist and novelist Zora Neale Hurston, who had also reported on the zombie myth, in particular pointing to

the medical aspect of the *bokor*'s rituals.

The next case to hit the headlines was that of Clairvius Narcisse, a man who had been pronounced dead in 1962 but appeared to have returned alive. Again, the man was thought to be suffering serious mental illness. However, an ethnobotanist named Wade Davis, who made a controversial study into the phenomenon in his 1985 book *The Serpent and the Rainbow*, showed that there was some basis to the idea of the *bokor* using potions to induce coma, and that the zombie myth, far from being a pointless invention, had an important function within Haitian society as a deterrent to anti-social behaviour.

······

ZOMBIES IN FICTION

One of the most famous examples of zombies in literature is the book *The Magic Island,* published in 1929. It was written by William Seabrook, a famous writer and explorer, and it was his reputation as an adventurer which lent some weight to his work. The themes of the book were black magic and most importantly, zombie labourers in Haiti, who he penned as working in the factories and cane fields owned by the Haitian-American Sugar Corporation. The book featured dark and brooding illustrations by an artist called Alexander King, which added a mystical element. The work made a lasting impression on the American public at the time of its publication, and reinforced the myth of zombies 'living' not too far from home.

···

THE HOLLYWOOD ZOMBIE

From these origins in Haitian folklore, the 'Hollywood' zombie of the screen developed. Instead of blue lips and a drugged stare, the modern zombie featured rotting flesh and open wounds, with a general focus on the gross aspects of physical decay. For

film-makers, this gory aspect of the zombie legend proved irresistible, and a slew of films followed, each one trying to outdo the next in terms of disgusting, repellent images. In the process, the films became humorous, not only glorifying the gore, but also parodying the entire horror genre.

····

STILL-WARM BRAIN

One of the major features of the modern zombie is its lust for human flesh. Instead of a zombie slave with no desire for life at all, the Hollywood zombie, as well as being a rotting corpse itself, enjoys eating live human beings. This gives immense scope for revolting, and sometimes hilarious, scenes, such as a zombie slicing the top off a victim's head and eating its still-warm brain. Other features of the horror zombie include tremendous strength, enabling it to pursue its victims tirelessly, without ever sleeping or needing to rest, and resisting all forms of attack, such as being shot, electrocuted, gassed or drowned. In addition, if one of its limbs are cut off, or it receives what would normally be a mortal wound, it carries on regardless, often with parts of its body dangling off. In particular, its head is capable of living without its body, and vice versa, leading to horrific — or comical — antics on screen.

····

ZOMBIE APOCALYPSE

Another contemporary feature of the zombie is that it belongs to a horde, giving rise to scenes in which the entire population of the 'undead' rise up in pursuit of the living. This perhaps addresses a central anxiety, or guilt, that in modern times, we are victims of our own greed, and that everything, or everyone, we have consumed and destroyed will, eventually, catch up with us and destroy us, too. This idea of a horde of reanimated corpses chasing after humans has become a 'new fear' in some circles. There is a genuine worry of a 'zombie apocalypse', whereby the dead rise up to fight the living, an event which will signal the end of the world.

····

THE ROMERO ZOMBIE

George Romero was a film-maker whose movie, *Night of the Living Dead*, released in 1968, brought a new genre to the screen. These films were extremely violent and disgusting, but they also offered an intelligent parody of modern society. For example, in his 1974 movie *Dawn of the Dead*, Romero set up an ironic situation in which victims barricade themselves into a shopping mall and are surrounded by every kind of luxury item, but unable to stop the slavering hordes of zombies who surround them, waiting to eat them alive in their palace of consumerism. It has been argued that Romero was also offering a critique of the horrors of war, in particular the Vietnam war, which was raging at the time his first zombie movie hit the screens, and which had, to some degree, inured the American public to scenes of extreme violence, in newsreels documenting the conflict.

Since Romero's time, the zombie movie has continued to thrive. The quality of the films remains, like every other horror genre, variable; however, among the celebrations of gore and bad taste, there are intelligent, amusing movies such as *Shaun of the Dead*, released in 2004. There has also been a spate of 'zom rom coms', based on postmodern 'mash-up' novels such as *Pride and Prejudice and Zombies*, as well as video games such as the *Resident Evil* series, which has sold millions of copies worldwide. It seems that the zombie legend is currently alive and well, and unlikely to die out any time in the near future.

VAMPIRE

The vampire, the immortal figure who stalks the night looking for innocent victims to plunge his pointed fangs into, is without a doubt the most notorious monster of today. This strange creature has a long and complex history, but perhaps what is most remarkable about the vampire is that it continues to fascinate people in the 21st century, addressing powerful issues of sexuality and death.

PAGAN ORIGINS

The origins of the vampire legend goes back to ancient times, when it was part of a pagan culture practised by Slavic peoples. In particular, the people who inhabited the Transylvanian forests elaborated the story, in what they called the 'old religion'. In the medieval period, the region adopted Christianity, but the rural peasants continued to observe their pagan customs, many of which were rituals to ward off the vampire. These people believed plagues, infectious diseases and other phenomena to be the work of the vampire, coming back as a revenant after death, to wreak revenge on the living.

The 'old religion' held that, after death, those who had suffered in life as a result of cruelty, or those who had committed hideous crimes, such as murder, would not rest in their graves, but were condemned to wander the earth for ever — alone. These people might include wronged lovers, abandoned pregnant women, prostitutes, thieves and violent murderers — indeed, all those shunned by society. As a result, it was thought, of their unlucky lot in life, the spirits of the dead became resentful, so got up out of their graves and went back to their villages, becoming walking corpses with evil intent. Their bodies were said to be swollen, and their rotting flesh gave off a sickening smell as they passed through the streets, looking for victims.

FRESH BLOOD

There was some basis in reality to certain aspects of the vampire myth. We now know that when a corpse is buried and starts the process of decomposition, it can sometimes begin to swell due to the action of particular gases. In some cases, this can cause blood to run from the orifices, blood which often appears unusually dark. It was known that corpses could spread disease, which of course is the reason for the age-old custom of burying them. Historians now believe that, to prevent disease epidemics, grave-diggers would often create mass graves to bury victims in. When they opened the grave to bury another victim, they would have seen some of the corpses rotting, and might well have panicked. These corpses, to them, would have looked as if they had come to life: a thin, emaciated, sick person who had recently died, might have become swollen and fat, and thick, dark, blood might be pouring from their lips and nostrils. Because of this, the gravediggers may well have assumed that the corpses had suddenly come to life, and not only that, had done so by

---

sucking the blood of the living (which would explain the apparently fresh blood seeping out of their orifices).

MEDIEVAL EUROPE

The medieval period in Europe was rife with vampire sightings. Indeed, these sightings quickly led to huge panics in some areas, where government officials were sent to quell the unrest. Priests were very much involved in the sightings, since it often fell to them to open up a grave where a vampire was suspected of lying. When they did, if they found that the body had grown fat, with rosy cheeks and fresh blood running from their mouths, as well as fingernails and hair that had grown long (another strange feature of the buried corpse), sheer panic often ensued. Their findings were often reported in the regional and national newspapers, usually in an extremely sensationalized account, so that an entire area or country could quickly be gripped by mass hysteria.

THE GOTHIC VAMPIRE

Given this extreme reaction, it was not long before the vampire legend found its way into popular literature, since it appealed so greatly to the gothic imagination. John Polidori, the physician of Lord Byron and Mary Shelley (author of the famous *Frankenstein*) wrote what is thought to be the first story of its kind, entitled *The Vampyre*, based on a fragment of a novel by Byron. In it, the vampire becomes a suave aristocrat, an altogether different creature from the stinking, bloating corpse of the medieval imagination. This transition of the vampire from an obviously terrifying monster to a polite, refined nobleman with a dark heart, who preys on high society, was hugely appealing to the public, and after its first publication, the story was reprinted again and again, as well

as being translated into many languages. A 'vampire craze' across Europe ensued, with influential writers such as Edgar Allan Poe, Alexandre Dumas and Nikolai Gogol, all writing vampire stories.

BRAM STOKER'S DRACULA

The vampire craze hit a new high with the publication of Bram Stoker's *Dracula* in 1897. The novel was written in the form of letters and diary entries, and told the story of an English solicitor, Jonathan Harker, summoned to the castle of Count Dracula in a remote Transylvanian forest. The Count asks Harker to come because he needs legal help with a property transaction, but once Harker is there, he finds himself prisoner in the castle.

BRIDES OF DRACULA

Harker meets three beautiful and seductive female vampires, the Brides of Dracula, and falls under their spell. Meanwhile, Dracula is busily tracking down Harker's fiancée, Mina Murray. The plot thickens, until a vampire expert, Professor Abraham Van Helsing, is called in. After the wasting illness of Mina's friend Lucy sets in, Van Helsing begins to suspect that a vampire is at work; and eventually, after many twists and turns, Mina herself is attacked by Dracula, but Van Helsing intervenes, coming to the rescue. In the final denouement, Harker kills Dracula by plunging a knife into his heart, according to time-honoured tradition of how to slay a vampire.

BIRTH ABNORMALITIES

Over the centuries that followed, the vampire legend was elaborated greatly, with many new features coming into play. Some of the old pagan beliefs remained; others, however, dropped away. It used to be thought that a baby born in caul was a vampire. Now we know that this is a perfectly normal occurrence. A caul is a membrane from the amniotic sac that separates a baby from the wall of its mother's womb. Usually, it ruptures during the process of birth, and today, is usually broken by the midwife or doctor, so that fewer babies are now born with this membrane covering them. In ancient times, the caul was thought to have special powers, and to bring good luck. It was believed to be a protection against black magic, to stop the bearer from drowning, and to enable him or her to make prophecies. However, in the medieval period, with the rise of the vampire myth, the caul took on a much more sinister significance, and would be destroyed as soon as the baby emerged. It was thought that the baby vampire would eat the caul, and then begin its search for human blood.

....

VAMPIRE TEETH

Babies born with teeth were also very much feared. Usually, when babies are born they display 'tooth buds', meaning that the teeth are still lodged in the gums, but in some cases, the teeth push through, and are called 'natal teeth'. Often, the teeth that come through first are the pointed incisors, giving the baby the appearance of a little vampire. In addition, birth abnormalities such as an extra nipple, hair on the body or birthmarks, all of which are quite common, would be taken as signs that the baby was a vampire. In these cases, the baby and its mother would be shunned, or even persecuted.

....

WARDING OFF THE VAMPIRE

Peasants traditionally used a number of items and rituals to ward off the vampire and keep it away from their homes. Holy water would be sprinkled over the threshold of the house, and strings of garlic would also be hung up,

in the belief that the vampire did not like the smell. Religious symbols, such as the crucifix and the rosary, were also thought to deter the vampire, as were poppy seeds, which were sprinkled around the grave of a newly buried corpse. Burying a body with a piece of iron in its hand, or placing a sprig of hawthorn in the coffin, was also claimed to prevent the corpse from coming to life and turning into a vampire.

....

SUPERSTITIONS

There were many other superstitions surrounding the vampire legend. For example, eating the remains of a sheep killed by a wolf could, it was believed, turn a person into a vampire. Those excommunicated by the church were also feared, because it was thought that the process might trigger this change. Prostitutes, alcoholics and criminals were believed to be particularly susceptible to vampirism, and for this reason, horrific mutilations were often performed on their bodies after they died. Piercing the heart with a wooden stake was thought to prevent vampirism, especially if the stake was made of rosewood or ash. The head and feet of the body might be cut off, and the head sometimes placed under the buttocks. The heart might be taken out, or a nail driven into the head.

....

SPECIAL POWERS

In different regions, there were varying beliefs about the appearance, character and behaviour of the vampire. In Bavaria, the vampire was said to sleep in its coffin with one eye open and its thumbs crossed. In other parts of Europe, vampires were said to walk the streets in their shrouds, to wear high-heeled shoes, or to be naked when they attacked their victims. In many regions, they were claimed to come out of their graves at night and return at dawn, when they heard the first cock crow. However, the idea that sunlight could kill a vampire was a later addition to the legend; in earlier times, the vampire was thought to take on the ordinary attributes of a human during the daytime, and only inhabit its supernatural form at night. In modern versions of the vampire myth, vampires often collapse or explode when exposed to sunlight, providing an exciting range of possibilities for the animators and film-makers of today.

Fear of water and fire is an essential vampire characteristic, as is the idea that the vampire has an over-sensitive sense of smell, explaining its aversion to garlic. Just as the vampire bat can sense the warmth of a victim's blood in the vicinity, through its heat sensors, so a vampire was believed to be able to smell the blood from a long way off. In some cultures, the vampire was believed to have an enhanced sense of vision, like an owl, and was able to track victims in the dark.

····

SILVER BULLET

Another strange feature of the vampire was its ability to turn itself into a number of animals, including foxes, bats, rats and moths. It might also have the power to control the minds of such animals. In addition, according to some versions of the legend, it could become a vapour, allowing it to slip under a door into a sleeping victim's chamber. It could also travel at immense speed, so that it could not be seen with the naked eye, and could quickly disappear from one place and reappear in another, like magic. The vampire might also be capable of hypnotizing victims before attacking them, depending on the victim's strength of will. It could withstand many forms of attack, including guns, knives and bullets. The only type of bullet that could kill a vampire, it was claimed, was a silver one. In fact, a corpse was sometimes shot with a silver bullet to prevent it rising up as a vampire at a future date.

Today, the vampire myth continues to grow in popularity, with fiction, film, and computer games exploring and elaborating the features of what appears to have become the scariest but most fascinating monster of all time.

A giant vampire bat attacks an old man suspended by his wrists. Medieval villagers believed that human sacrifices could ward off evil spirits.

EASTERN SPIRITS

Eastern cultures have their own versions of the primarily European phenomenon of the vampire. The Hindu 'Vetala', for example, is a demonic creature that inhabits cemeteries; and the Yurei is a Japanese spirit that comes to life when a person dies an unhappy or violent death.

....

THE VETALA

The Vetala inhabits corpses, causing all manner of trouble to communities, but also, in some instances, guarding those same communities from attack. Like the vampire, the vetala is the spirit of a dead person trapped in the zone of the undead between life and afterlife.

....

CRAFTY DEMON

The vetala can sometimes be repelled by chanting holy mantras, and by performing proper burial rites for the corpse they inhabit. According to legend, the vetala may be captured by a sorcerer, and used to prophesy the future, or to understand human nature. However, it is difficult to catch a vetala, since they are sly, crafty demons. To illustrate this, the story is told of a king who tried to capture a vetala who was living in a tree in a cemetery. He knew that the only way to do this was to lie in wait for it, keeping quiet so he would not be detected. But each time he did so, the vetala would begin to tell him an entrancing story that ended with a question. The king would not be able to help himself from answering it, and so he never managed to capture the vetala.

....

THE JIANG SHI

The Jiang Shi is another form of Eastern spirit, originating in China. Legend has it that during the day, the Jiang Shi hides in dark places such as caves, or hides in a coffin. At night, it comes out, and begins to hop, with its arms stretched out in front of it. Like the vampire, it seeks out human beings, killing them to suck out their life force and, as a result, sustain its own survival.

The Jiang Shi is the spirit of a recently deceased person, and can be reanimated by magic rituals, by the corpse being struck by lightning, or by a pregnant cat jumping over the coffin. One gruesome belief is that, after death, the body simply does not decompose. As in the West, observers in ancient times noted that the corpse's hair and fingernails sometimes appear to grow after burial. However, the reason for this is, as the body decomposes, the skin retracts, causing the hair and nails to look longer. As with the vampire myth, it was thought that the restless spirit may belong to a person who has committed suicide, a person who had died a violent death, or someone who has been wronged in life.

....

WARDING OFF THE JIANG SHI

The Jiang Shi resembles the zombie of Western horror movies, in that it has rotting flesh and greenish-white skin. The Jiang Shi is also in a state of rigor mortis, which is why it holds its arms stiffly in front of it, and possibly why it hops. In addition, the Jiang Shi

has long white hair. There are many methods of warding off the Jiang Shi when it appears: showing it a mirror, because the Jiang Shi is frightened of its own reflection; throwing vinegar over it; piercing its skin with a sword made of peach wood. If the Jiang Shi hears a cock crow, it will withdraw of its own accord, knowing that day is approaching and it must scurry back to its coffin or cave before sunrise.

····

THE HOPPING JIANG SHI

The origin of the 'hopping' Jiang Shi is thought to date back to a practice whereby those who died far away from home were transported back to their villages of origin by tying the corpses to a long rod of bamboo. When the bamboo was carried along, by two people at each end, the corpses would appear to hop, as the bamboo flexed. Another source of the legend is thought to derive from a folk belief that Taoist priests could teach corpses to hop back to where they were born, to save their families the expense of hiring wagons to transport them for burial. The priests were said to drive the corpses at night, since it was considered bad luck for the living to look at the corpses. This practice often took place in the province of Xiangxi, giving the Jiang Shi their name.

···················

THE YUREI

The yurei is a type of Japanese ghost, or spirit, that comes to life when a person dies a violent or unhappy death. It is believed that when the spirit or 'reikon' leaves the body it must wait until the funeral rites are performed so that it can join its ancestors, and continue to protect the living family. If these rites are not performed, whether due to a violent death, or due to powerful negative emotions such as hatred, jealousy, and revenge, the spirit becomes a yurei, haunt-

ing the living until the conflict is resolved. In appearance, the yurei resembles a traditional ghost, dressed in a white burial kimono, and sometimes with a white piece of cloth tied around the head. The yurei has long black hair that looks rather unkempt, and its hands flop from the wrists as if lifeless or broken. The yurei seems to have no substantial body, floating in the air, and is sometimes accompanied by two ghostly flames, in colours such as purple, green or blue.

Japanese mythology classifies many kinds of yurei, for example 'onryo', which are ghosts who seek revenge for a wrong sustained in their lifetime; 'ubume', mothers who died during childbirth may return to care for their children; 'funayurei', the ghosts of people who died at sea, and who may be covered in fish scales; 'zashiki-warashi', the ghosts of those who died as children, and who are mischievous rather than dangerous; and 'samurai' ghosts, who died in battle. These warrior, samurai ghosts, unlike most of the other yurei, have legs, and are often portrayed as strong and full of life.

····

REVENGE FOR MURDER

The yurei are said to come out at night, between two and three in the morning, and to haunt places near where they died or were killed. In most cases, if the wrong done to a yurei is righted, the yurei will cease its haunting. However, there are some particularly powerful yurei, such as the vengeful onryo, who never cease to haunt the living, even when their quest is successful. These yurei are believed to be particularly numerous on Mount Fuji, where many people, over the years, have committed suicide.

According to Japanese tradition, the best way to get rid of a yurei is to help it resolve its problem, whether that is the performance of traditional burial rites, or the righting

of a wrong done to it in its former life. For example, if a person died as the result of murder, the yurei would be likely to demand that its own family take revenge on the perpetrator. Other methods of banishing or calming the yurei include placing 'ofuda', holy Shinto scriptures, on the ghost's forehead, or placing the ofuda over the threshold of the family house, to prevent the yurei from coming in.

Illustration from *Vikram and the Vampire*, a collection of Hindu tales by Richard Francis Burton (1821–1890).

CIHUATETEO

The Cihuateteo are figures in Aztec mythology. They are the souls of women who have died in childbirth, and are revered as fallen warriors that perished in the battle of labour. They can traverse the earthly realm, the celestial and the underworld, passing between each world with ease. Their job is to escort the souls of the noble deceased to the afterlife, but at night they take on another task entirely.

FALLEN WARRIOR

The deities of the Aztec tradition were usually associated with blood, suffering, war and death. They believed that blood was essential to appease the gods, and as such, any person who died in a form of battle, would be revered. This belief extended to childbirth, and a woman who did not survive labour would receive the same admiration as a man who had died in battle. The souls of these women, however, were named the cihuateteo, and were seen as very dangerous characters indeed.

LURKING IN THE SHADOWS

The cihuateteo were tasked with escorting the spirits of dead and honourable warriors to the afterlife, a noble role which is a complete contradiction to their night-time activities. Under the cover of darkness, however, the cihuateteo would leave their home in the sky and escort the sun to set in the West. They would then take their place at a crossroad — a location commonplace in vampire legends throughout many cultures — hiding in the shadows, and prey upon men and children. They were known to be capable of inflicting entire communities with illness, and could command the spreading of disease. Mental illness was often attributed to the cihuateteo, as it was believed they were able to enter the mind of a person and make physical changes. One of their tricks was charming men into committing adultery, and then keeping them as sex slaves. The cihuateteo had a penchant for luring children away from their mothers, presumably to replace the child they did not live to know, and to torment innocent mothers with feelings of grief and despair.

WORSHIP

In the ancient Aztec myth, spirits and deities visit the mortal realm every 52 days in the Cholq'ij calendar. The cihuateteo were worshipped as ancestors of Cihuacoatl, a goddess of fertility and motherhood (another figure of duality: both seductress and goddess). In another Aztec belief system, the cihuateteo were believed to be emissaries from Mictlan, the lowest level of the underworld. Despite a fear of the cihuateteo, they were still venerated. Whether this was through admiration at the sacrifice they had made through childbirth, or through simply attempting to keep the spirits happy, is not clear. Shrines were built at the crossroads they were believed to haunt, and offerings of corn and bread were left for them. Children were advised to stay inside on these days, however, and men were warned not to communicate with mysterious women.

....

SKULL MOTIF

The cihuateteo are most often represented in ancient reliefs or modern art surrounded by skull motifs. The evil spirits are often depicted with skeletal faces, wearing a skull headdress, a necklace made of human bones and having sharp, clawed feet. They are usually shown kneeling at a skull altar and referred to as guardians of the afterlife. Sometimes human hands form a garland round their necks, and often they are pictured with their mouths wide open, exposing sharp teeth with which they tear flesh to pieces. The belief that they could seduce men suggests they were able to magically alter their appearance to become attractive, but they are most often represented as being hideously ugly.

STRIGOI

A strigoi is a vampire-like creature from Romanian mythology. In the graves of the deceased, a body may turn from human to strigoi, and with this hideous transformation comes an insatiable thirst for human blood and an uncontrollable urge to kill.

A ROMANIAN VAMPIRE

When the deceased turns from human corpse to strigoi, it becomes a predatory beast, concerned only with consuming human blood for sustenance. It only comes out at night, resting all day in its grave. It has the ability to turn itself invisible, and will often enter the house it lived in and throw items about, causing the residents to become frightened. It can also transform itself into different forms, such as animals. They are also able to use their powers to disguise their chalky white skin and the blood-red rings that encircle their glowing yellow eyes, and appear attractive. They use this opportunity to seduce mortals into allowing them to drink their blood. The strigoi is blood-thirsty, but also consumes its victim's soul, which it sucks out through the mouth, ears or nose. In some versions of the myth, the strigoi feeds upon its victim's heart, and this gives it strength. Legend has it that the strigoi is also capable of causing disasters including floods, droughts and storms. It is believed that they do not like sunlight, and if they enter churches or other 'holy places' they will burn until there is nothing left but a pile of ash.

....

BECOMING A STRIGOI

Once a person is dead, there are several ways the corpse might transform into a strigoi. Initially, the use of garlic as a preventative measure was sometimes implemented. During the burial ceremony, in some regions, it was traditional to place garlic sparingly around the grave, inside the coffin and sometimes

inserted into the mouth of the dead. This would decrease some of the likelihood of a transformation, but there were other reasons a strigoi might take over a corpse. If a person dies and has never been married, there is a huge risk of that person becoming a strigoi.

····

STRIGOI SPOUSE

In this instance, the family of the deceased would arrange for the corpse to be quickly wed to an unmarried person of the same age, in order to prevent the dead from becoming a strigoi. This was a risky move, however, as sometimes it would not work, and the deceased would return from the grave as a strigoi, regardless. The strigoi is likely to search for its new spouse and attack its family, angry at its unwanted transformation. If this happens, the undead must be stabbed through the heart with a sickle, and put back in its grave. It was also believed that cats, like in other mythologies around the world, possessed supernatural or magical powers. If a corpse was walked over by a cat prior to burial, then the deceased was likely to become a strigoi. To stop this happening, the corpse should be buried with a bottle of wine. Six weeks later, the wine should be dug out of the grave and consumed by the deceased's closest relatives. This process stops the deceased from emerging as a strigoi, and prevents the relatives from becoming a strigoi when they pass away. Legend also has it that, if a strigoi drinks the blood of its victim, and then forces the victim to drink strigoi blood, that would result in the victim transforming.

Once a dead person has become a strigoi, there are ways of stopping it from being physically able to lift itself out of the grave. If the body is pierced in multiple places with a needle or a sickle, this will stop it being able to rise out of the grave. In addition to

this, coins or candles placed in the corpse's hand will have the same effect. In the event that a strigoi is seen struggling to get up, if hemp is burnt and the smoke is wafted around the grave it will cause the monster to become weak and helpless.

····

KILLING A STRIGOI

There are believed to be four main methods of killing a strigoi. Once it has been exhumed from its grave, the classic technique of driving a stake through the heart is most effective. Ideally, the stake should be fashioned from wild rosebush or aspen wood. It should be driven at the heart in such a way that it pierces the organ and the stake fixes it to the earth. If it attempts to rise out of the earth, it must be set alight as quickly as possible. Decapitation, removing the heart and burning it or simply burning the entire body are also ways of destroying a strigoi. In some versions of strigoi folklore it is believed that the creature has two hearts, one of which is where its vitality is stored. It is this heart which spurts out blood when it is torn apart by the stake.

····

SEVEN YEAR RULE

According to the legend, if a strigoi is not killed within seven years after its original burial, then in its seventh year it can, once again, take on the appearance of a mortal (while remaining a strigoi) and re-establish itself in society. At this time, it will have lost all its predatory urges, and can lead a relatively normal life. Often, it will move to another region, where it cannot be identified and can start a new life. However, every Friday night it will need to rest in a grave in a cemetery, and will not rise again until Sunday morning. If a strigoi procreates with a mortal, it would result in a 'normal' baby, that would, unfortunately, live forever as a vampire, after death.

GHOST

A ghost is mostly conceived of as being the spirit or soul of a deceased person. After death, some believe that the essence of that person leaves the body, and remains on earth to haunt the living. Often, this spirit is charged with negative emotions, and will spend eternity reeking havoc on mortals.

THE SEANCE

A belief in the existence of ghosts is prevalent in many cultures around the world. They often vary in appearance and behaviour across different traditions, but generally they are always thought of as an apparition of a deceased person. In some cultures the ghosts are honoured, either through a fear of their capabilities, or a desire to appease them. In the West, they are not revered particularly, and over the years the belief in them has steadily declined. Around the 19th century there was a strong belief that ghosts were real and could be contacted. Seances became popular, and people would often enlist the services of a medium to perform them. During these sessions, the spectators would sit around a table, and the medium would enter into a trance, allowing a spirit to take over his/her body. The medium would then communicate the thoughts of the spirit, sometimes taking on the deceased's personality and voice. There has always been a certain degree of doubt surrounding the authenticity of the seance, however, they remained a popular practice for some time.

....

WALKING THROUGH WALLS

A ghost is made up of 'nothing', it is an intangible mass, and is often depicted in art as having a hazy or smoky appearance. It can walk through walls, pass through objects and appear and disappear at will. It often haunts the location at which it died, and will scare people away if it pleases. In reported encounters, a ghost that can be seen will often resemble the person who died, and somewhat gruesomely it may even appear still afflicted with whatever killed that person. A famous ghost that is said to stalk the halls of the Tower of London, is Anne Boleyn. She has been seen numerous times, always at night, and always with her severed, bloody head neatly tucked under her arm.

....

THE POLTERGEIST

A ghost cannot always been seen, but can often be 'felt' to be present. It can give a person the feeling of being watched or touched, and in this instance, it can cause a person to feel uneasy and scared. This type of ghost has the ability to pick up and throw objects, and is known as a 'poltergeist'. Reports of poltergeist attacks have been recorded in many countries, with encounters dating back centuries. Often, in a building in which someone has died, the spirit will remain, and strike fear into the inhabitants by knocking on walls, opening and shutting doors and violently throwing furniture about. There have even been instances where people have experienced being pushed, thrown, picked up and generally attacked by an invisible force. The poltergeist is able to cause maximum chaos in this role and as it cannot be seen there is no way of stopping it, tracking it or knowing when it will strike. This figure has gone on to inspire many works of fiction, perhaps most famously the 1982 Tobe Hooper film *Poltergeist*.

．．．．

UNFINISHED BUSINESS

A popular plot device in fiction involving ghosts is the notion of unfinished business. Whether this stems from a genuine belief or not is not clear, but it is generally thought that a soul can become trapped on earth if a person has died through murder or suicide. Traditionally a person that commits suicide is not believed to be accepted into the after-life, and as such remains on earth in a state of limbo. This troubled soul would haunt the location in which it took its life, and spend eternity in turmoil over its own actions. A person that was murdered obviously died an unhappy and premature death, and this spirit would seek out revenge on the living. Often in fiction this act would result in the spirit being able to 'cross over' to the afterlife.

．．．．

THE BHOOT

In India, there is a fear of the 'bhoot'. They are believed to be restless souls that have had trouble trying to reach the afterlife. Often this is due to a deceased person not being buried according to traditional burial rites, or if the person was murdered. A bhoot is not like the traditional concept of a ghost in that it is able to take on the form of a human or an animal. However, identifying a bhoot in whichever guise it assumes is easy — if its backwards-facing feet are visible. In many Indian traditions the earth is considered to be a semi-sacred land, and so while bhoots are trapped in this realm, they will not physically touch it, instead floating just above the ground. Like the Western ghost, the bhoot will haunt the location in which it was killed, and will become protective of this area.

．．．．

THE CHURAIL

The soul of a woman that died during pregnancy or childbirth is known as a 'churail' — a different type of bhoot. A churail has the appearance of a human woman, but with facial features which are upside down. Like the traditional bhoot, the churail also has feet which face backwards. Like the siren of mythology, the churail can transform into a form which is irresistible to men, and use this power to lure them to their death. The bhoot and churail are dangerous entities, and are unlikely to ever successfully cross over to the afterlife.

．．．．．．．．．．．．．．．．．．．．

GHOST FESTIVAL

The Hungry Ghost Festival is a good example of how a culture celebrates and positively welcomes the dead. On the 15th day of the 7th month in the Chinese calendar, it is widely believed that the dead travel from the underworld to earth. They return in a ghost form and walk amongst the living, visiting relatives. This day is called Ghost Day, and is celebrated by Chinese people all over the world. The entire month is spent honouring the dead, and this is done by offering the spirits items such as food, jewellery, money and clothing. In the family home, the dinner table is piled high with food and one seat is left empty for the returning spirit. Out in public, in places such as theatres, the front rows are left empty for the ghosts, and concerts are performed for their entertainment. In the streets, temporary altars are constructed and filled with food offerings. The festival is concluded by the locals creating paper lanterns, and setting them on the water. The lanterns are watched as they drift away, and when the lights go out it is believed the ghosts are back in the underworld.

The Ghost of the 'Brown Lady' on the staircase of Raynham Hall, Norfolk, England.

An engraving by Gustave Doré from an 1860 edition of *Dante's Inferno*. Dante with his guide Virgil are addressing a ghost in 6th Circle of Hell.

WITCH

If you refer to a dictionary you will be informed that a 'witch' is a woman who is believed to have magical powers — powers that are sinister and evil. She is usually portrayed in books and fairy tales wearing a long black cloak and a pointed hat, travelling everywhere by broomstick. She is kept company by her faithful black cat and a smouldering cauldron, in which she concocts her evil spells, but above all she is feared and hated — the devil in the form of a woman.

A WITCH IN HISTORY

Feared by young and old alike, witches have been hunted down and executed throughout history. Witches are always women and it was once believed that because they were the 'weaker sex' they could easily be seduced by the Devil himself and carry out his evil deeds. This rather contradicts the meaning of the word 'witch' which in fact means 'wise woman'; dispelling the theory that they were stupid and gullible. They certainly are not stupid when it comes to plotting their evil deeds. A witch is nearly always portrayed as being ugly with long, tangled black hair, a rather over-sized nose, often adorned with a wart, extremely long fingernails at the end of long, wrinkled fingers, a pointed chin and a wan or rather sickly pale complexion. She has the ability to fly, appears to have no warm feelings to mankind and seems to be incapable of producing tears. This was put down to the fact that she is so shrivelled and dried up in both body and mind that it was impossible for her to produce enough liquid to show this emotion. A witch is ageless, and many believe they are being reincarnated from a previous despot or inhumane character that was unable to pass peacefully into the next world. Whether tall and thin or short and fat, the witch has been feared throughout history because of her innate ability to perform evil spells.

WITCHES FROM THE REFORMATION

So where exactly did it all start? Witch-hunts reached their pinnacle in the 15th century in Europe and North America, covering the great periods of upheaval during the Reformation and the Thirty Years' War. Witches were relentlessly pursued and executed for being akin with the Devil, and this hatred resulted in up to 60,000 deaths. Even Joan of Arc was associated with witches when she was condemned as a witch on 30 May 1431, despite the fact that centuries later she was declared a saint, but because she claimed to have heard 'voices' compelling her to carry out missions for her king, she was burned at the stake. Her adversaries were fully aware of her superhuman powers but put them down to the fact that she was in touch with the Devil, not God as she claimed. Not many of the witches put to death during this time fitted the description of the witch as we know her today.

PAYING FOR HERESY

If we go even further back into history we can see that the persecution of witches was a strong bone of contention with the Church. Pope Gregory IX authorized the killing of witches as far back as the 1200s and declared that anyone who supported their beliefs would be tried for heresy. Despite the order coming from such a high power, witches were more or less left to their own devices, that is until 1484, when Pope Innocent VIII issued a charter stating that witches did actually exist and, as a result, church authorities killed and tortured hundreds of thousands of women. They were subjected to inhumane torture just to get them to admit that they flew through the night sky, had sexual relations with demons, took the form of animals and practised black magic.

PAGAN WICCA

The word 'witch' comes from the Old English word 'wicca', which has become synonymous with pagan religious rituals and consequently associated with witchcraft. Because many of the wicca symbols can be confused with satanic icons, such as the Pentacle, the Chalice, the Cauldron and the Wand, they are seen as the primary tools of the witch. Wicca also became associated with not only this world but the afterworld too, and subsequently became a direct challenge to the Christian church. Many old religious manuscripts have some rather interesting if not comical remarks regarding wicca or witches. For example, a christian would kneel in worship whereas a witch would stand on their heads to worship their 'master'; purely a hypothetical belief on behalf of the Church.

WITCHES' HAMMER

One of the most famous documents to have ever been written about witches was by two Dominican monks by the name of Jakob Sprenger and Heinrich Kramer, published under the title *Malleus Maleficarum*, or Witches' Hammer. It was a work that rivalled any modern-day science fiction film in its content and detailed descriptions of what a witch *actually* was and what they *actually* did. It would appear that celibacy had distorted the monks' image of what women were like and stated that:

> All witchcraft comes from carnal lust, which is in women insatiable ... they collect male organs in great numbers, as many as twenty or thirty members together, and put them in a bird's nest.

Of course this description of the already tainted reputation of the witch added fuel to the fire and their persecution was heightened. In fact, the *Malleus Maleficarum* became the preferred text on how to deal with witches, and those who took part in the Inquisition — a Roman Catholic tribunal for discovery and punishment of heresy — seemed only too pleased to inflict the punishment as recommended by the authors. Apart from being asked to look closely for the 'Devil's mark' which could be detected by prodding the offender with a sharp object, they were also told to search for the purported 'witches' tits' — a third nipple with which they allegedly suckled the Devil. If any of the interrogators became aroused while carrying out these inspections, it was believed to be the work of the devil manifesting itself through the witch. Needless to say many of the alleged 'witches' eventually confessed, unable to bear the nature of some of the tortures. In some places whole villages would be wiped out because the entire female community were deemed to be witches. Witch hunts were not restricted to just Europe, though, they even touched the shores of America and, just like the trials in Europe, the situation got out of hand.

LEGENDARY WITCHES

There are few cases of accused witchcraft that stand out as being quite momentous due to the alleged witch's position in society:

· · · ·

JOAN OF NAVARRE (1370–1437)

Joan of Navarre was the wife of King Henry IV of England. She was accused of being a witch and trying to bring the downfall of the king by her black magic. In 1419, her stepson, King Henry V, suddenly had Joan arrested and imprisoned in Pevensey Castle in East Sussex. He accused her of being a witch and attempting to poison his father through her evil spells. She lived in fear of her life for three years, knowing only too well that witches were burned at the stake. However, her stepson seemed to have a pang of conscience when he himself faced death in 1422. He set her free and granted Joan a full pardon.

· · · ·

ANNE BOLEYN (1507–1536)

Unable to bear her husband, King Henry VIII of England, a son, Anne Boleyn was accused of being a witch by her frustrated spouse. What made it worse was that she bore a sixth finger on her right hand, which was believed to be a sign of a witch. Henry wasted no time in having her beheaded, frightened of what evil incantation she would cast upon him.

· · · ·

CATHERINE MONVOISIN (c. 1640–1680)

Catherine Monvoisin, also known as La Voisin, was a French midwife and to many who knew her, a witch. It was around this time that several members of the aristocracy were executed for witchcraft and poisoning in the Affaire des Poisins. She was most certainly a practitioner of medicine and provided abortions for many unfortunate young women who had nowhere else to turn. But it was the love powders and potions that she created using ingredients such as Spanish-fly, bones of toads and teeth of moles as well as the fact that her lover was a magician and she had been known to assist a Parisian priest in the dark arts which helped confirm people's belief. Even though she was frequently visited by famous Parisian women who could not get enough of her love potions, she was burned at the stake in 1680 in an effort to put an end to her devious misdeeds.

· · · ·

SALEM WITCH TRIALS

The most famous of the American witch hunts was the episode that became known as the Salem Witch Trials which took place in 1692. It started when a few innocent girls befriended a slave woman by the name of Tituba, who had a reputation for casting evil spells. They became bewitched and started acting strangely — screaming hysterically, having convulsions, foaming at the mouth and howling like wolves. The area in Massachusetts where this took place was extremely Puritan and people were convinced that these young girls had become possessed by demons, put there by the witch herself. Tituba was condemned as a witch, along with several other people who it was believed worked in collusion with the Devil. Between the months of June and September, 19 men and women were all convicted of witchcraft, carted to Gallows Hill, a place infamous for hangings just outside the village of Salem, and executed. Another man, believed to be in his 80s, was crushed under a heavy stone for refusing to stand trial, while hundreds of others languished in jail.

MODERN-DAY WITCHES

One could be mistaken in thinking that these are events that happened in the distant

The Witch of Berkeley, 852. It was said by William of Malmesbury that this witch was exhumed by her friend the devil who took her away on his horse.

past, and yet in 1976 a woman in Germany was ostracized by her community for being a witch. She was stoned and her animals were slaughtered while she stood by and watched helplessly. In 1981 a woman was stoned to death in Mexico because they believed she had cast a spell which resulted in an assassination attempt on the Pope.

Today, people are still persecuted for being witches, mostly older women but more disturbingly young children who are cast out of their families, abused and, in many cases, murdered. Just one example is in the Democratic Republic of the Congo where it is believed as many as 50,000 children live on the streets of the capital, Kinshasa, unable to go home because they have been accused of witchcraft. There are witch camps in Ghana where it is thought as many as 2,000 elderly women live in destitution, forced to live there for decades.

The Witches' Sabbath
Francisco Goya

El Aquelarre (*The Witches' Sabbath*). The Black
Paintings is the name given to a group of
paintings by Francisco Goya from the later
years of his life between 1819–1823. They
portray intense, haunting themes, reflecting
his fear of insanity and old age.

CRETINOUS CRYPTIDS

TALES OF MYSTERIOUS figures abound in various mythologies and cultures all over the world, but cryptids are a special type of monster. Cryptids are beings which have been sighted countless times, but are generally not considered to be real; dismissed due to a lack of concrete proof or through academic rationale. However, there are some people that continue to investigate these elusive beasts, and celebrate any evidence uncovered. In the field of cryptozoology, infamous characters such as the Loch Ness Monster and the Yeti are searched for, in an effort to prove their existence to the disbelieving scientific community. But to the people living where these stories originated, a fear of the cryptids is perpetuated through repetition of the tales. In New Jersey, a dense woodland named Pine Barrens is believed to be home to a horned-devil. While many may doubt its existence, it does not stop some searching for the beast at night.

BIGFOOT

One of the most intriguing cryptids of all time is the elusive Bigfoot, a huge ape covered in dark hair, between 6–10ft (1.8–3m) tall, who walks like a human being. He is also known as Sasquatch, from a Native American word meaning 'wild man'. It is claimed that he lives in the forests of the Pacific north-west of America. Despite his existence being unproved, there are those that still search for him and monitor the woods, hoping to catch a glimpse.

WILD APE-MAN

Bigfoot gets his name from the enormous footprints he is said to leave behind. Casts of his footprint have been made that measure eight inches wide and 24 inches long. Most of the casts have five toes, like a normal ape, but some have two, three, four or six. The creature is claimed to have a low-set forehead, a large ridge on the brow, and a crest on top of the skull, much like a gorilla. It has also been reported that the beast exudes a stench, which can be smelled from a long distance away as he walks along.

For many years, there have been myths and legends about the 'wild man of the woods' that inhabits the north-west area of the United States and Canada. The Native American tribe known as the Lummi, from Washington state, tell of 'Ts'emekwes', a great monstrous being stalking the forests, while others describe the 'Stiyaha', a large, hairy ape-like creature with hair that ranges from brown to golden. Other names for Bigfoot include 'Kwi-kwiyai' and 'Skoocooms'. Legends of monstrous creatures are also common in many other cultures around the world, and appear to be a reoccurring theme in folklore from many countries. Perhaps the most famous of these, along with Bigfoot, is the Yeti, otherwise known as the Abominable Snowman.

EVIDENCE FOR THE BEAST

There are many gruesome tales about the activities of these primitive beasts. Among some communities, the rumour was that they were a race of wild cannibals with supernatural powers, and that they were known to carry off humans, especially children, to kill and eat. Families living in or near the woods described close encounters with the creatures, and even attacks on their property, but nobody could prove without doubt that they existed.

During the 1950s, people in the area began to try to collect scientific, observable evidence of Bigfoot. A series of individuals came forward with photographs and plaster casts showing the huge footprint of the creature, and the story was soon taken up and sensationalized in the press. After much excitement, many of these stories were found to be hoaxes, but other evidence could not be so easily explained.

THE PATTERSON-GIMLIN FILM

In 1967, a film was put forward purporting to show the capture of the creature. This film, which became known as the Patterson-

Gimlin film, intrigued many scientists, and for some time had a great deal of credibility among the public. However, it was finally denounced by the majority of scientists as a hoax, they claimed that the creature shown in the film was a man dressed in an ape costume. Nevertheless, there are those today who still believe that the film is genuine, and consider the media's spin on the story as a deliberate cover-up, perhaps ordered by the government. There are websites dedicated to the beast, where fans detail their encounters, post photographs and discuss this woodland celebrity with other enthusiasts. Today, it has been established that most of the alleged Bigfoot sightings, that is, between 70–80 per cent, are entirely false. However, there are some that have not been so simple to discount. Among the scientific community there are individuals who have advanced tentative theories as to what, if it does exist, the creature might be.

PREHISTORIC APE?

These include a prehistoric animal called Gigantopithecus, an extinct type of ape, fossils of which have been found in China. Anthropologist, Grover Krantz, believed that the animal could have migrated to North America across land masses that are no longer in existence. However, critics have pointed out that Gigantopithecus walked on four legs, and the Bigfoot is said to walk on two. Other theorists have suggested that a surviving Neanderthal man may be the real identity of the Bigfoot, but since no remains of any such species have been found in the Americas, this seems doubtful.

Yet there have been scientists who regard the search for Bigfoot as a valid endeavour, including Jeffrey Meldrum, a professor of anthropology, and primatologist, John Napier. Others, such as Jane Goodall,

considered to be the world expert on chimpanzees, are broadly sympathetic to the idea of a cryptid race of giant apes. In 2002, she remarked laughingly in a radio interview, 'Maybe they don't exist, but I want them to'.

YETI

The Yeti, aka the Abominable Snowman is a cryptid believed to stalk the Himalayan regions of Nepal, India and Tibet. He is thought of as a counterpart to the North American Bigfoot, and is just as elusive. The indigenous people of the region have always known of the Yeti (from the Tibetan for 'little man-like creature'), as the creature is part of their history and mythology. Throughout the area he is known by many names, some of which translate to: Wild Man, Snowman, Man-Bear and Man Eater. It was not until the 19th century that he became known in the Western world.

METOH-KANGMI

In 1889 a British army major reported seeing a large footprint in the snow. There were many other witnesses to this footprint but no evidence was collected from it. Some speculated it was a standard footprint which had melted and so naturally enlarged, resulting in an unusually formed print. In 1921, a second British army expedition were camping out on a mountain in the Himalayas. A few of the men noticed some dark figures in the distance, and so they quietly moved towards them, hoping to identify them. The figures soon disappeared, but more unusual footprints had been left in their wake. The next morning they asked their guide about their experience, and he replied that they had seen the 'metoh-kangmi', words which can be translated to 'man-bear' and 'snowman'. From this term the Yeti received its new nickname in the Western world – Abominable Snowman.

RED EYES

There have been many alleged sightings of the Yeti over the years. Generally, he is believed to be between 6–7ft (1.8–2m) tall, covered in brown and red hair, with a conical head, large teeth, deep-set eyes which glow red and elongated arms which hang below his knees. He is said to run on all fours but walk upright. According to the indigenous people of the region, he smells terrible, and you can often smell him before you can see him.

THE YETI TODAY

Although the existence of the Yeti is generally doubted, there are some believers who actively search for the beast regardless. Because of this, pieces of 'evidence' pop up from time to time, but these are often dismissed as hoaxes. In 2011, a video showing the discovery of so-called Yeti footprints and hair in Russia was released to the media. This evidence was found during a trip to the remote mountains of Kemerovo. The scientific community has yet to reach a conclusion on this report.

A frame from a cine film of Bigfoot, taken by Roger Patterson, 1967, at Bluff Creek, Northern California, USA.

CHUPACABRA

The chupacabra is one of the strangest cryptids in modern times. Its appearance has been described as similar to both a reptile and a dinosaur. It has a row of spikes along its back and tail and is covered in coarse, leathery, green skin. It hops about on its back legs like a kangaroo and, if disturbed, will hiss and screech at a decibel which is unbearable to humans. The beast exudes a horrible, sulphuric smell and if fixed by its glowing red eyes, a wave of nausea will overcome its victim.

GOAT SUCKER

In the 1970s, near the town of Moca, Puerto Rico, a vampire-like creature had reportedly begun to kill sheep and goats on the hillsides. Farmers noticed that the bodies of the animals had been drained of blood through small puncture wounds around the neck and chest: clear indicators of a vampire-like attack. Because of these strange incidents, the mysterious creature roaming the hills became known as 'El Vampiro de Moca'. There were also rumours of a Satanic cult in the area, who were believed to emerge at night to perform gruesome ritual killings on livestock. However, no more information about such a cult was forthcoming, despite repeated investigations.

The name chupacabra was coined by Silverio Perez, a Puerto Rican TV entertainer. He was referring to news reports of a creature that had apparently killed eight sheep in March 1995 in a place near the town of Canovanas. The sheep were found dead, each with three puncture wounds at the neck. According to a resident of the area named Madelyne Tolentino, the culprit was a bizarre-looking animal that she had seen one day from her garden. She had, reportedly, attempted to capture it, enlisting her husband's help, but the strange creature had become frightened and had managed to get away.

....

FEAR OF THE FANGED CREATURE

Another witness in the area, a student named Michael Negron, reported a 'dinosaur', as he called it, with large fangs coming out of its mouth, and a row of spikes down its back. A hunt for the strange beast was launched, but it was never found. Nevertheless, the residents of the area continued to believe that it was roaming the area, killing livestock, and considered that it may next begin to attack humans. Thankfully, this never came about, but it was enough to frighten parents to keep their children from walking about freely in the countryside.

....

COUNTLESS SIGHTINGS

Over the years that followed, sightings of chupacabras, or accounts of their destructive behaviour, were reported in Honduras, Chile, El Salvador, Brazil, Bolivia, Argentina, Panama and Nicaragua. In July 2004, the legend of the chupacabra reached the United States when an animal was shot by rancher Devin McAnally in Elmendorf, Texas. It was identified, at first, as a Mexican hairless dog, or possibly a wolf-coyote cross. However, a more far-fetched theory was that it was the product of a botched animal experiment and had escaped from a laboratory.

Since the carcass of this strange creature was available for inspection, a number of experts were able, for the first time, to take a look at the 'chupacabra'. It was an ugly creature weighing 9kg (20 lb), and its skin was blue and hairless. Eventually, through DNA testing, it was established that the 'monster' was a coyote suffering from a severe form of mange. The creature became known as the 'Beast of Elmendorf'. During the next few weeks, two more suspicious-looking creatures were picked up in the area, both suffering from a bad case of mange. Both animals were also identified as coyotes.

....

MANGE-RIDDEN COYOTE

Despite some professionals discounting the existence of the chupacabra due to their discovery of mange-ridden coyotes, odd reports of drained dead animals continued to surface. In Russia, reports came of overnight killings of sheep and turkeys, while in Maine, USA, there were similar stories about attacks on chickens. In all cases, the animals had been bitten and drained of blood through small puncture wounds on the neck. A woman living in Texas then found three strange animal corpses near her farm. She cut off the head of one of these, and put it in her freezer for later identification. Later, she

reported it to the authorities and the press. It looked like a hairless dog with fangs and big ears. She believed it to be a chupacabra that had been killing her chickens, but the state mammalogist, John Young, disagreed. According to him, it was a grey fox with sarcoptic mange. Later, it was identified as a coyote, using DNA analysis, but many were doubtful, since the head looked so unlike any coyote they had ever seen.

....

THE 'ALIEN RACE' THEORY

Among cryptozoologists, there is a rather fantastical theory that the chupacabra may be what is known as an 'anomalous biological entity', otherwise known as an ABE. These are hybrid animals created by a race of aliens who are able to synthesize the genetic data of different organisms, thereby creating a 'monster'. The theory is that these creatures, intended to live on extraterrestrial planets, have somehow escaped and now inhabit the earth.

The chupacabra, the infamous blood-sucking creature said to inhabit parts of the Americas.

LOCH NESS MONSTER

Of all the cryptids in modern culture, the Loch Ness monster, or 'Nessie', as it has affectionately become known, has attracted the most attention from scientists and academics. Most are sceptical about its existence, yet in the field of cryptozoology, there are those who believe that the creature is a surviving relative of a prehistoric plesiosaur. Its appearance is generally recorded as being the size and shape of a sea serpent with a very long neck; however, these accounts vary, as does the evidence gathered in photographs and sonar readings over the years.

....

LEGENDARY MONSTER

The earliest legend about the Loch Ness monster is the story of St Columba, the Irish monk, written in the seventh century. St Columba was travelling in the land of the Picts, as a missionary hoping to bring Christianity to the pagan hordes, when he came across some men burying a man beside the river Ness. The man had, according to their account, been killed by a monster in the river. The dead man's boat was tied up on the other side of the river, so St Columba ordered a servant to get it back. On the way, the monster reared out of the loch and tried to kill the servant. St Columba called on God, made the sign of the cross, and the monster retreated, vanishing beneath the waves.

The first modern sighting of the creature took place in May 1923, when Alex Campbell, a man responsible for the policing of Loch Ness, reported in the local newspaper that he, and several others in the area, had seen a 'monster' in the loch. Ten years later, the paper published a news item about a tourist, George Spicer, who had seen what looked like a prehistoric dragon crossing the road towards the loch. The dragon was excessively long, he claimed, with an undulating neck, and was carrying its prey in its mouth. Many letters to the paper followed, from people claiming that they, or their relatives and friends, had spotted the monster, describing it as a dragon, a sea serpent, or a monstrous fish. The creature soon became known as the Loch Ness monster.

....

THE 'SURGEON'S PHOTOGRAPH'

In the 1930s, there were several photographs of the monster that attracted great speculation. One of these was what came to be known as the 'surgeon's photograph', taken by a respected British surgeon who refused to be named. This showed a sea serpent with a long neck, rising out of the loch. Years later, in 1984, an article in the British Journal of Photography analyzed the photo, and found that the neck and head were only about four foot long. In 1994, it was revealed that the photograph was a hoax. In reality, the monster was a toy submarine with a plastic head and neck. It had been built by Christian Spurling, the son-in-law of a big game hunter, Marmaduke Wetherell, who had previously been found to have falsified evidence regarding the monster. Many years before, Wetherell had been sent by the British tabloid newspaper the *Daily Mail* to travel up to the loch and find the monster. He found what he said were tracks of the beast, but it later transpired that he had made these with a dried hippo's foot, of the kind used at the time for umbrella stands. Spurling admitted what he and Wetherell had done in 1984 shortly before his death at the age of 90.

....

THE DINSDALE FILM

In 1960, Tim Dinsdale, an aeronautical engineer who worked in the Royal Air Force, travelled to Loch Ness to find the monster. On 23 April 1960, he claimed to have seen a large creature swimming in the loch, and grabbed his camera to film it. The film shows the monster swimming across the surface of the lake, showing its hump. Many believed this was proof of the monster, though some criticized it, saying that the outline could have been a boat or other vessel. Dinsdale himself gave up his career in the RAF, and devoted the rest of his life to proving that the monster existed. However, he never came up with incontrovertible proof during his lifetime.

In 1993, when a documentary was made on the subject, the film was enhanced, showing a series of smaller humps. This led some people to believe that Dinsdale's film was indeed accurate, in that the enhanced version showed what could have been the outline of a plesiosaur. Further footage came to light in 2007, when lab technician Gordon Holmes took a video of a 'jet black thing, about 45 feet long', moving in the waters of the loch. The video was broadcast on television, but some doubts were cast on Holmes' credibility, since he had previously claimed to have filmed fairies.

SONAR INVESTIGATION

In addition to sightings and photographs, Nessie has also been the subject of sonar investigation. In 1970, the American Academy of Applied Science, headed by Dr Robert Rines, launched an investigation into the loch, using automatic cameras and sonar equipment to monitor activity within it. Two years later, an underwater camera showed pictures of what appeared to be a large flipper, measuring 6—8ft (1.8—2.4m) long. The fin was a diamond shape, suggesting that it could have been that of the prehistoric plesiosaurus. However, some critics argued that the photograph had been re-touched, and that the original was too unclear to identify the shape as a fin.

One of the team members in investigation, Peter Davies, told that one night he was out in a small boat on the loch when he detected what he took to be the monster, moving under the boat. He reported that the 'echo trace' of his sonar equipment showed a huge animal only 30ft (9m) below him. He admitted that he had found the experience very strange, not to say terrifying.

....

THE 'GARGOYLE HEAD'

In 1975, the team found what they thought was further evidence of the Loch Ness monster. This was what appeared to be a 'gargoyle head', and, although the image was very unclear, it looked as though Nessie's face was in view. However, a later expedition to the loch found that the image was, in fact, that of a tree stump in the water.

Sonar research into the phenomenon has not, to date, yielded firm evidence of the monster living in the loch. In 1968, a team led by Professor D. Tucker of the University of Birmingham tested a new type of sonar device in the loch, mounting it beside the lake so that it would detect any objects passing through its beam. During the fortnight

Artist's impression of the Loch Ness Monster after numerous sightings of the cryptid in 1934.

that it was there, it recorded a great deal of unusual activity, such as animals 20ft (6m) in length passing in front of it. The professor consulted with local fisheries, but found that there were no fish of that size in the loch. He concluded that the sonar device may have recorded the 'fabulous monster' of legend. Another researcher, Andrew Carroll, from the New York Aquarium, used sonar equipment to cover the loch, and again found traces of an animal about 20ft (6m) in length. Since then, these objects have never been positively identified.

BIRD-LIKE CHIRPING

Other scientists and cryptozoologists have investigated the loch to find out whether the monster lies beneath it. During the 1960s, a biologist from the University of Chicago built a system of underwater microphones at the loch, hoping to hear sounds from the monster. He reported 'bird-like chirping', and a series of knocking and clicking noises, along with a swishing noise that he thought could be the sound of an animal swimming in pursuit of its prey. The sounds appeared to stop whenever a boat passed on the loch, and

SEEN BY MISS JANET FRASER & TEN OTHER WITNESSES FROM "HALF-WAY" TEA HOUSE, AULTSAYE, SEPTEMBER 22ND, 1933, 11A.M. (FROM A DRAWING MADE UNDER HER SUPERVISION)

SIDE VIEW OF HEAD. SHINING SPOT.

HEAD TURNED TOWARDS WITNESSES.

HEAD TURNED AWAY

to resume again once the boat had disappeared into the distance.

In recent years, efforts to find the monster have continued. In 2004, the BBC sent an expedition to probe the Loch from end to end, using 600 sonar beams. There was no sign of a large animal in the water, of the type fitting the description of the Loch Ness monster. A small submarine sent to investigate the depths of the lake yielded no further information. However, the search continues.

····

THE PLESIOSAUR THEORY

Some commentators have argued that a single plesiosaur, or similar creature, could not live in the loch alone, but that there must be a breeding population of monsters there. Estimates range from about a dozen to 100 individuals. These commentators point to photographs which appear to show several of the creatures together. There is no consensus to date on what type of animal the monster is. Some believe it to be more like a mammal, such as a primitive type of whale known as a zeuglodon, or a manatee. There have also been suggestions that the monster is in fact a long-necked seal, as yet unknown to science, a giant otter, an oversized sea slug or even a massive eel.

There is much debate over the issue of whether, if the monster is indeed a plesiosaur, it could survive in the cold waters of the loch. Some believe that this would not be possible, though recent studies have suggested that certain dinosaurs, and possibly the plesiosaur, were warm-blooded creatures. Sceptics also point to the fact that an air-breathing animal such as a whale or plesiosaur would have to come up to the surface of the water to breathe, and therefore would be much more visible than the monster, at present, appears to be. In addition, questions have been asked about the food source for the

monster. The loch has a supply of fish but, critics of the theory argue, this would be nowhere near enough to feed a population of large, warm-blooded aquatic creatures.

····

UNDERWATER WAVE

Other explanations for the phenomenon have been advanced, including the theory that the sightings have been caused by an underwater wave. Such waves, known as seiche, sometimes gather momentum within a bounded area of water such as a lake. They are caused by wind pushing an area of warm water to one end of the loch, forcing the cold water to the other end, and causing a wave as a result. The wave occurs underwater, so that it is not visible on the surface, but causes a swelling movement that could, possibly, push debris to the surface so that it resembles the hump of a large animal. Another theory, advanced by zoologist and popular writer Dr Maurice Burton, is that the 'monster' is in fact a log. He suggests that pine logs may have fallen into the lake and begun to decay, causing gas to build up inside the wood. The gas cannot escape, because it is sealed in by the tree's resin, but eventually, it ruptures and the log is forced to the top of the water, where it might perhaps look like a large animal swimming along the surface.

Whatever we make of these different theories, it is certainly true that the mystery of the Loch Ness monster is still one that intrigues many investigators, whether from a scientific perspective or not. The fact that there have been many hoaxes over the years has obscured the various perspectives surrounding the debate, but it seems that today, we are no nearer to finding out the truth about whether Nessie, the Loch Ness monster, really exists.

JERSEY DEVIL

In the dense woodland of Pine Barrens, New Jersey, lurks a creature with a devil-like tail, the hooves of a horse, large wings, sharp claws and glowing red eyes. It is believed to be a harbinger of doom, and has historically appeared to locals before times of disaster. The legend of the Jersey Devil has survived for over 250 years, and while today its existence is doubted, in the past there was a deep-rooted fear of the beast.

DEVIL CHILD

The story goes that in Pine Barrens, United States, in 1735, a woman named Japhet Leeds was due to give birth to her 13th child. She lived with her family in extreme poverty, and the prospect of having another mouth to feed was too much to bear. It is believed that in a moment of sheer panic she exclaimed, 'I don't want any more children! Let it be a devil.' Legend has it that when the horribly deformed baby was born it somehow delivered itself, crawling from the womb and escaping into the woods via the chimney. It is believed to have fed on livestock and local children out playing in Pine Barrens. This is the most well-known and accepted tale of how the Jersey Devil came into existence, but there are others. In one story, Japhet Leeds angered a gypsy, who cursed the baby with physical abnormalities. Another claims Leeds was a witch and God cursed her pregnancy as a result. Some believe the baby was born human but somehow transformed into a demon voluntarily.

····

BANISHED FOR 100 YEARS

In 1740 the Devil was allegedly captured and exorcised. The ritual banished the creature for 100 years, and in 1840 it returned, around the time sightings started to be documented.

Of all the local encounters a famous one sticks out: Joseph Bonaparte, brother of Emperor Napoleon, claimed to have been out hunting and ran into the Devil. Newspapers started recording the sightings at the advent of the 20th century. One of the first ever documented reports of the Devil was in 1899 when a Philadelphia newspaper covered the story of George Saarosy, a man who woke in the night due to high-pitched screams coming from his garden. He got to the window just in time to see the Jersey Devil swoop past and off into the night.

····

'PHENOMENAL WEEK'

In the decade following the Saarosy account, rumours of the Jersey Devil continued to circulate around New Jersey, Philadelphia and Delaware, and then something extraordinary happened in 1909. During the week of 16–23 January, literally thousands of unusual encounters were reported to the police and the press, sparking mass chaos. The accounts were largely harmless ones, but it is probably the quantity of them which terrified the local population. Freakish footprints were discovered and alleged sightings of the Jersey Devil were reported, and consequently chronicled in local newspaper *Philadelphia Record*. This was a huge story and was soon picked up by the national press, though it was largely ridiculed. The *Philadelphia Record* dubbed this Jersey Devil rampage as 'Phenomenal Week', and to this day it is believed that January is the best time to spot the Jersey Devil, 21 January being the most common day for sightings. The panic in January 1909 was so immense that workers stayed at home and schools were closed. Dozens of animal mutilations were reported during this time, with farmers' livestock being torn to pieces by the creature.

····

EYES OF THE BEAST

One of the 1909 accounts was that of a New Jersey resident, Zack Cozzens. On 16 January, at the beginning of the flurry of alleged encounters, he reported seeing the Jersey Devil on a roadside. He was first alerted to it due to the high-pitched hissing sound it made. He managed to get a good look at the creature and went on record as saying, 'Something white flew across the street. I saw two spots of phosphorus, the eyes of the beast. It was as fast as an auto.' That same night, it was spotted in Pennsylvania.

Soon after, a couple witnessed the Devil sitting on the roof of their shed. Terrified, they phoned the police, who arrived promptly and shot at it to no avail. A prominent city councilman reported hearing a hissing sound at his back door one evening. When he went to investigate he opened the door to discover a pair of cloven hoofprints embedded in the snow, hoofprints which continued to be reported in the local area. After the madness of January 1909, accounts gradually started to dwindle until they ground to a halt in 1926.

····

TWENTY-FIVE YEAR GAP

A quarter of a century then passed by, with locals still telling the story of the bizarre creature in the woods, and children being too afraid to pass through them alone. Then, in 1951, a 10-year-old boy's story brought the Devil back to everyone's attention. He claims to have seen the Devil at his bedroom window 'with blood dripping from its face'. Several days later, the same creepy hoofprints started to appear again, hissing sounds were waking people at night and otherworldly screams were heard coming from the woods. Reports poured into the police stations and the officers were frustrated at having to deal with this case again.

····

POLICE INVESTIGATION

One investigation by the police yielded a result which gave them the ammunition to set the story straight to the locals. They discovered a stuffed bear paw attached to a stick and figured some prankster was using it to create these unique hoofprints. The police produced signs saying: 'The Jersey Devil is a hoax', and hung them across highways and in shop windows. This only served to spur on the locals to bear arms and march into the woods with the intention of apprehending the Devil themselves. The police arrested several of the vigilante 'leaders' in the hopes it would deter others from taking the law into their own hands.

In 1966, a man named Steven Silkotch opened his shed to discover his poultry livestock had been decimated. Incredibly, the two German Shepherds that lived in the shed had also been torn to pieces. Silkotch reported this incident to the police and the press and it became the last story both organizations treated seriously.

····

THE JERSEY DEVIL TODAY

Encounters with the Devil today are rare, but that has not stopped people regularly venturing into Pine Barrens and searching for it. The locals keep the story alive; children are warned about entering the woods at night, much like in the legend of the Bogeyman. Areas of the woodland have special aspects of the myth attached to them. Leeds Point, New Jersey, for example, is believed to be where Japhet Leeds' house was located, the place where the Devil was born and quickly escaped from. Those that believe the creature is dead claim to know the site where the body is buried. There are many stories told to this day of the Jersey Devil, and despite how much they vary and despite the lack of hard evidence, there is no doubting that something really did terrorize Pine Barrens 100 years ago, and that earlier still, something dark and evil really was lurking in those woods.

MOTHMAN

In the winter of 1966 a series of strange happenings spooked the residents of Point Pleasant, West Virginia, USA. The town was gripped with fear when sightings of a tall figure with large wings and glowing red eyes started to be reported. As investigations into the phenomenon began, more bizarre and unsettling occurrences were uncovered.

15 NOVEMBER 1966

An abandoned TNT plant, situated six miles north of Point Pleasant, was the setting for the first sighting of, what was to be dubbed, the Mothman. The plant complex is made up of several buildings, which are connected by underground bunkers and tunnels. During World War II the facility was used to store and supply TNT for America's war effort, and although it is not used for this purpose now, an eerie atmosphere remains there. On that cold November's evening, a couple were driving past the building when they became aware of a pair of large, red eyes looking at them. They slowed the car down to try and work out what they were looking at, and what was looking at them, and as their eyes adjusted to the dark they realized the eyes were attached to a figure between 6–7ft (1.8–2.1m) tall, with large wings folded against its back. Suddenly it moved, and the driver slammed down on the accelerator. As they fled down Highway 62, at a speed of 100mph, it appeared next to the car, flying alongside them with its enormous wings outstretched. When they reached Point Pleasant they had lost the creature and, despite being scared, turned back to look for it. As they approached a cornfield, they felt something on the roof, and then the grey figure appeared in front of the car. They shone their headlights on it and, again, saw the pair of terrifying red eyes. The creature seemed uncomfortable in the light, and scurried off. They drove back to Point Pleasant and immediately alerted the authorities. Deputy Sheriff Millard Halstead took their statement, and while they were there the police station's phone rang. There had been three more sightings of the Mothman.

····

THAT SAME EVENING

At 10.30 p.m. Newell Partridge, who lived 90 miles away from Point Pleasant in Salem, was at home with his dog, Bandit. He was watching television when it seemed to switch off by itself. The screen was dark for a few seconds, and then an odd pattern appeared. At the same time, an unusual sound could be heard coming from outside, like the whining of a generator as it winds up. Bandit went nuts at this point, barking to be let outside to investigate and protect his owner and territory. Partridge grabbed a torch, and stepped out onto the front porch. Bandit was howling at the hay barn, and so Partridge shone his light onto it, wondering if it could be kids out there messing about. As the light hit the barn, a pair of red eyes stared back at him. They filled him with terror. Bandit tore across the yard and Partridge went inside to retrieve his gun. He was then struck by a feeling of dread, and simply could not leave the house. The next morning he realized Bandit had not come home, and he never saw his dog again.

·····················

16 NOVEMBER 1966

Rumours of the previous night's events started to circulate around Point Pleasant, and people began to worry. A press conference was held in the county's courthouse on 16 November 1966. Deputy Halstead repeated all the witness statements to the media, who quickly gave the creature the name 'Mothman', after a character from the *Batman* television series. The same night, the Thomas family saw a red light in the sky

that seemed to move and hover above the TNT plant. Marcella Bennett was driving to the Thomas house and was spooked by the same red light in the sky. When she arrived at the house, she got out and then picked up her baby. Out of nowhere, a grey figure rose before her, as if it had been lying on the ground. It towered over her and her daughter, with its large glowing red eyes piercing into her. She was so shocked, she dropped her baby on the ground, and as she bent to pick her up the creature disappeared. She hurried into the Thomas house and soon panic spread across the household. Suddenly something was heard shuffling about on the porch, and red eyes could be seen peering in through the windows. Ralph Thomas called the police but by the time they arrived, the Mothman had gone. Marcella was so traumatized after this that she had vivid nightmares for weeks, and had to see a therapist to help her come to terms with her encounter. At night she claimed to hear what sounded like a woman screaming out in the woods, and she was convinced it was the Mothman haunting her.

······················

JOHN KEEL

The author John Keel heard about the happenings in Point Pleasant and decided to come and investigate for himself. He had a keen interest in the supernatural and paranormal, and wrote many books on UFOs and theories of mysterious strangers appearing to historical figures in the forms of ghosts, aliens, monsters, demons and angels.

Keel became fascinated by the Mothman case, and compiled an impressive list of over 100 witness statements dated between November 1966 and November 1967. Largely, the descriptions of the creature were similar. Most agreed it was between 6–8ft (1.8–2.1m) tall, was far wider than a man, its eyes were positioned almost at its shoulders, and it had bat-like wings which allowed it to fly somehow gracefully — gliding rather than frantically flapping. All agreed on its eyes glowed red and it had murky dark skin.

....

STRANGE SOUNDS

What differed was the sounds it was heard to make. These varied between a hiss, to a hum, to a screech and even a scream. Keel noted these different attributes down and then turned his attention to odd electrical interferences which had also been reported at this time. He noted that from the fall of 1966, there had been several accounts of televisions seemingly switching themselves off and then the screen being filled with a bizarre pattern, and returning to normal minutes later. Phones would cut out for no reason and then strange crackling sounds would be heard on the line. When the phone company was questioned they would report no faults and come to no logical explanation. The area around the scene of the first sighting, the TNT plant, continued to be the scene of peculiar paranormal phenomenon. Red lights were often seen over the facility, and those that dared to drive past it at night would find their engine would cut out for no reason, leaving them stranded. Around this time, there were even reports of suspected poltergeist activity. Several households claimed to hear odd thumps in the night, hear scratching sounds outside, and witness locked doors suddenly flinging open and slamming shut of their own accord. One family who lived half a mile away from the TNT plant left the area entirely, so bad were the disturbances they experienced. Keel had a theory that all of these unusual happenings were somehow connected to the Mothman.

15 JANUARY 1967

In the new year, Mary Hyre, a Point Pleasant correspondent for the Ohio newspaper, *Messenger*, started to put together a feature on the Mothman encounters. Her phone number was given to local residents who soon bombarded her with calls; one weekend she received over 500 witness statements. One evening Hyre was working late in her office when a short man wearing thick glasses turned up unannounced. He asked Hyre for directions to a town in West Virginia, and as he spoke in a low, monotonous tone she felt him draw himself closer to her, his hypnotizing eyes just visible through his thick glasses. Suddenly uncomfortable with the situation, she got the attention of her manager, who joined them in the office. The man's behaviour was odd, he seemed otherworldly and despite them giving him the directions he allegedly came for, he seemed to want to stay in the office. He then picked up a pen from a desk, and studied it like it was some unknown object. Bizarrely, he then laughed at it and ran out of the building, leaving Hyre and the manager stunned. A few weeks went by and the man appeared again. This time it was out in public and Hyre spooked him. He realized he was being watched and ran down the street towards a black car which he got into and then sped away.

15 DECEMBER 1967

Reports of the Mothman declined around the end of 1967, but Point Pleasant was soon back in the headlines. At 5.00 p.m. on 15 December, Silver Bridge, which linked Point Pleasant to Ohio, suddenly collapsed, sending dozens of vehicles to the depths of the Ohio River. Forty-six citizens were killed, but only 44 bodies were recovered. This tragic event was considered by some to be connected somehow to the Mothman, and to this day the disaster is tarnished with superstition.

...

ANOTHER ODD ENCOUNTER

The same month, another peculiar little fellow showed up at the office of Mary Hyre. He was dressed formally, and Hyre was quite fascinated by him because he had abnormally high cheekbones, narrow eyes and an accent that she could not pin down to any country she knew of. He was interested in local UFO sightings and Hyre allowed him to look at her file of press clippings. He was furious that she would not talk to him about this subject directly, and she got so frustrated with him she kicked him out of her office. That evening she got reports that all the witnesses that had seen lights in the sky were visited by the same strange man, who pressed each of them for more information.

MOTHMAN MYSTERY CONTINUES

There is no explanation for what took place in Point Pleasant. It could be that the creature was imagined, and that the hysteria that gripped the town caused others to believe they had seen the legendary Mothman. It could be that the creature was simply an owl, with eyes that reflected brightly when light hit them. The so-called poltergeist activity could have been imagined, too, along with the lights in the sky. John Keel believed the creature was real. He also believed that Point Pleasant was a 'window' area, a place where strange occurrences such as mysterious 'men in black' figures appear from nowhere, where spine-chilling sounds are heard and cannot be traced to a source, and where monstrous beasts with glowing red eyes stalk humans at night.

The Mothman, reportedly seen a number of times in the Point Pleasant area of West Virginia, USA.

THE BEAST OF BRAY ROAD

Between 1989–1992 in the United States, a series of sightings of an unusual creature took place in the Wisconsin towns of Delavan and Elkhorn. A large, frightening animal was spotted multiple times. Witnesses estimated it was 7ft (2.1m) tall, as wide as a bear and with canine or wolf-like features. Its eyes were said to glow yellow and its body was covered in thick, matted hair. Reluctant to admit a werewolf may exist, cryptozoologists have put the Beast of Bray Road in the Bigfoot category.

WISCONSIN WEREWOLF

There had been rumours of a werewolf in Wisconsin since encounters were reported in 1936, 1964 and 1972, but then there was a gap until 1989. The sightings then started up again, and at quite a pace. The werewolf was named the 'Beast of Bray Road' due to most often being seen in that vicinity, however, encounters that take place anywhere from northern Illinois to southern Wisconsin are attributed to the same animal from Bray Road. The first encounter involved 26-year-old bar manager Lorianne Endrizzi. She was driving along Bray Road one evening after work when she saw a figure kneeling on the pavement. Unsure what it was, she slowed down and passed it by, trying to work out what it was. Suddenly, it looked up and revealed its pointed fangs, yellow eyes and long, wolf-like face. Endrizzi slammed on the accelerator and drove away as fast as she could. When she got home she wrote down the features of the beast she had encountered. One very unusual attribute was that the creature was completely covered in dark hair but had human-like fingers, with claws on the ends. In that moment she had also noticed the beast seemed to be holding food in one hand, completely unlike any animal she had ever seen before. She did not know if she had seen a man or a beast, but she was completely shaken up by the experience.

HUGE FOOTPRINTS

In the same year there were another two reported encounters. A dairy farmer in Elkhorn named Scott Bray (coincidentally) claimed to have seen a 'strange looking dog' in his pasture which was situated near Bray Road. He said it was exceedingly large and tall, seemed to be rather muscular, and was covered in matted grey and black hair. He could see the creature's ears were pointed and that it had a long, hairy tail. The creature did not attempt to attack him, it simply turned and ran away. Bray followed the beast but he disappeared into the long grass of the pasture, leaving behind a set of deep and oddly-shaped footprints in the mud.

LUCKY ESCAPE

The next encounter also took place in Elkhorn. Russell Gest saw the beast around the same time as his neighbour, Scott Bray. Gest was out walking along a wooded path when he heard the sound of twigs snapping and leaves rustling. He suddenly felt nervous and looked around anxiously. It was then that the creature emerged. Gest thought it looked like an oversized dog, with a big, thick neck and wide shoulders. It stood on its hind feet and attempted to walk. It wasn't very steady on its feet, and seemed to wobble as it took steps towards him. Gest figured now was a good time to run and so sprinted off. He looked back briefly and saw the beast was now on all fours. Gest was always unsure why the creature did not follow him, but whether he was really in danger or not, he considered that day to be his lucky escape.

· ·

MARCH 1990

The next sighting happened at the beginning of the 1990s. Mike Etten, a dairy farmer in Elkhorn was out at 2.00 a.m. strolling down Bray Road after an evening drinking with friends. He maintained in his statement that he was not inebriated, but of course this casts some doubt on his story. Under the glare of the moon, Etten spotted a dark-haired creature sitting by the roadside, in the same way Endrizzi had spotted it before. It was eating something with its paws, and again, holding the piece of food in a much more human-like manner than animal. As Etten passed the creature, it lifted its head. He saw its snout, its thick and wide head, its covering of thick, dark hair. Etten's reaction was a surprising one. He was not scared, he simply assumed the animal was a bear and went on his way. It wasn't until he caught wind of other sightings that he realized what he had really seen.

CHRISTMAS 1990

Eleven-year-old Heather Bowey was next to report an encounter with the Beast of Bray Road. She was walking along Loveland Road with some school friends when they saw a large dog walking along a creek. The children were excited to see it, and tried to entice it over by calling to it. It was then that the beast stood up on its hind legs, scaring them all witless. As before, it struggled to walk on its back legs, and so dropped down onto all fours. The terrified children then ran as fast as they could, with the beast in pursuit. They made it to Heather's house which was nearby, just in time to turn back and see the beast run off in another direction. Heather commented to her mother that the beast took, 'bigger leaps than dogs run'.

· · · ·

COMMUNITY SPIRIT

These reports were eventually picked up by the national press, none of whom took it seriously. Because of the negative attention, the witnesses started to feel ridiculed. In the Wisconsin towns of Delavan and Elkhorn, the residents positively embraced the story that was making their towns famous. Teenagers held werewolf-themed parties and merchandise was produced to sell to tourists hoping to catch a glimpse of the beast. Although the locals largely made a joke of the situation, underneath all the merriment, there were underlining concerns and a palpable feeling of fear and anxiety within the community.

· ·

FEBRUARY 1992

The wife of Scott Bray, Tammy, had a run-in with the beast late one night in the February of 1992. She was driving home from work when a dog-like animal suddenly sprang from the bushes and ran into the path of her car. She slammed on the brakes just at the right moment, and as the car screeched to a halt the creature stood, rooted to the spot. To her horror, the headlights revealed the 'dog-like animal' really had little in common with a domestic dog. It had a broad chest which was covered in thick, grey and black, matted hair. It stood on its hind legs for a minute or so, then all of a sudden dropped down onto all fours. It had pointed ears, a narrow nose, a thick neck and glowing yellow eyes. Another minute passed and as the lights of another car approaching appeared in the distance, it sprinted off into the woods. Tammy Bray rushed home to tell her husband that she had seen the same creature.

OCTOBER 1999

In the years following Tammy Bray's encounter, the beast was hardly seen. Then, seven years later, on Halloween night, Doris Gipson of Elkhorn was driving along Bray Road after work. She took her eyes off the road for one second to change the radio station when she felt her front right tyre go over something. Assuming she had hit a squirrel or similar, she pulled over to have a look. There was no wounded critter in the road or damage to her tyre, so she opened the car door to get back in. Suddenly, she became aware of a dark form speeding towards her from the woods, and could hear heavy footsteps getting louder and louder. She got into her car, turned the key in the ignition and was about to put her foot on the accelerator when this 'form' leapt onto her trunk. She could not see what it was, but being from Wisconsin she knew it was the Beast of Bray Road. It was thrashing about on top of her car and then suddenly slipped off. Seizing her opportunity to get away, she sped off towards home.

CURIOSITY

Later that night, however, her mind couldn't focus on anything other than her experience on Bray Road. Despite still being shaky and frightened, she was also extremely curious to see the beast again and so decided to revisit the scene. When she got there, she pulled over by the road and waited. An hour or so went by and she felt her patience running out. She was about to set off home when from the corner of her eye she saw movement. The creature was prowling around on all fours, stopping occasionally to sniff the grass like a dog. She noted the sheer size of the beast, and how it was built in a similar way to a muscular man. Satisfied she had seen enough, she started to drive away. As she left Bray Road she peered up into her rear view mirror, to see a pair of glowing yellow eyes staring back at her from the darkness.

Today, the beast is not seen very regularly. Some say the beast is really a wolf, a coyote or some kind of hybrid animal. Whatever the truth of the beast is, Bray Road is a stretch of highway treated with extreme caution, and avoided by some at night.

A lycanthropic forest demon said to have been captured in Germany between 1531–1661. This creature was said to inhabit forests around Salzburg and Hamburg. It was perhaps a witch wearing an uncured skin, a primitive rite which could have given rise to the werewolf legend.

A kraken or giant octopus attacks a
French sailing vessel (1802).

A ship attacked by a sea serpent in the Sea of Darkness. A hand-coloured woodcut from *History of the Northern Peoples* by Swedish writer Olaus Magnus (1555).

FOUKE MONSTER

In Miller County, Arkansas, USA, some believe that a Bigfoot-like creature lives in the woods. Unlike other cryptids of this type, the Fouke Monster is known to be hostile. He is said to be 6–10ft (1.8–3m) tall, to weigh between 180–360kg (400–800 lb) and to be covered in thick red hair. In reality, there is little evidence to support the claim that such a creature exists, however, a plaster cast of a three-toed footprint from 1971 continues to intrigue monster hunters and tourists alike.

THE MONSTER ATTACKS

In 1971, the Ford residence in Fouke was the scene of the first sighting of the monster. One night at around midnight, Elizabeth and Bobby Ford heard someone walking around on their porch, leading them to think there may be an intruder on the prowl. Bobby went outside and investigated, but could not find anyone hanging around the property, so went back inside and locked the door. The next night, the same thing happened at around the same time, midnight. The next evening, Elizabeth was home alone while Bobby was out on a hunting trip with his brother, Don. She was napping on the couch and awoke when she felt a breeze fall over her. She looked at the clock and saw it was midnight. Suddenly, a hairy arm came through the window and tried to grab her. Elizabeth struggled to stay out of its reach, and scrambled away from the window. She looked up at the creature, which she had at first believed to be a bear, and saw its red eyes, which she later described as looking like 'coals of fire'. It was in this moment that Bobby and Don arrived home, and spotted the creature from the rear of the house. It ran away from the house and into the field, and the men shone their torch on it. Bobby

and Don had weapons on them, and began to shoot at the monster. They thought they'd managed to land a bullet in it when they saw it collapse to the ground, but they wanted to see the fallen beast for themselves, so they started to walk towards where they believed it was laying. From the house they then heard Elizabeth screaming, so they rushed back, with Don in the lead. Bobby was walking up the steps onto the porch when a hairy arm came over his shoulder and wrestled him to the ground. He was pinned down by the monster, and Bobby looked into his bright red eyes, absolutely terrified. Somehow, he broke free and managed to escape his clutches. He ran into the house, screaming about what had just happened. Elizabeth, Don and Bobby looked out the window and saw the monster running off into the fields and disappearing out of sight.

THREE-TOED FOOTPRINT

The following morning, the Ford family inspected the outside of the house for evidence of the attack. They discovered scratch marks on the front porch and by the window, and most importantly of all, they found a large three-toed footprint measuring 13.5 inches long embedded in the ground. That night, the story spread throughout Fouke, and interest grew in the Ford's nocturnal attacker. At least 100 people looked around the grounds of the Ford house, and in the fields surrounding it, searching for clues. A plaster cast was made of the footprint, and experts examined it, hoping to identify what kind of creature it could be, but a conclusion was not reached. In the late 1970s, the cast was burnt in a fire, destroying the one piece of evidence pointing to the creature's existence.

••••

THE SECOND SIGHTING

The Ford family lived in fear of the monster returning, but it never did. However, three weeks after their experience, another couple saw the beast, but it behaved in a totally different fashion. Mr and Mrs Woods were driving along the highway when they saw a creature run across the road, right in front of their car. The windows were down and they could smell a disgusting odour. The creature appeared to be hunched over, yet was running as upright as it could. It had long, dark hair and though it was bent over a bit, it was obvious that it would be enormously tall if it stood up straight. As it moved, its arms swung by its sides like a monkey, and for a second the couple considered it could be some kind of primate. But then it turned and looked at them, and they saw its red eyes beaming at them. It then bolted off into the woods, at a speed so fast that the couple couldn't think of any human or animal capable of moving so quickly.

••••

APE-LIKE CREATURE

The couple reported their story to the police, and a few days later there were more sightings of the same ape-like creature. Witnesses were telling the same story of a tall figure, hunched over and fast moving, covered with red hair and with glowing red eyes. Around

this time, further strange footprints were discovered, but none were photographed as evidence. The police decided to search for the beast, and sent dozens of officers out to investigate the sites where the monster had been seen. In some areas, the dog units deployed with the officers would pick up a scent and then refuse to follow it. However, the search yielded no results.

Today, Fouke is proud of the legend attached to it, and became world-famous in 1973 when the story of the Ford's encounter was adapted for the big screen. *The Legend of Boggy Creek* grossed over $22 million and since then scores of movie goers and monster hunters have visited Fouke, Arkansas, looking to separate fact from fiction.

A cast of a footprint said to belong to the Fouke Monster.

Hell
Chapman Brothers

English visual artists, the Chapman Brothers work together as a collaborative sibling duo. Their sculpture installation *Hell* (2000) consisting of a large number of miniature German Nazi figures was part of the Saatchi collection destroyed by fire in May 2004.

Section Six:

POPULAR CULTURE

BOOKS AND FILMS FEATURING monsters are incredibly popular with audiences, and have been since they first started being produced. It seems that there are a few key works of fiction that are responsible for the entire monster movie genre ever being created. Mary Shelley's 1818 novel *Frankenstein* signalled the zombie movie with its reanimation of a corpse; Bram Stoker's 1897 classic *Dracula* resurrected the vampire and spawned many films on the subject; and Robert Louis Stevenson's *Jekyll and Hyde* (1886) highlighted the duality of man, an idea which links to the figure of the werewolf. Beyond this, ancient mythological beasts, demons from hell, terrifying sea serpents and critters from folklore provide the inspiration for the stories that keep the legends alive. As long as audiences like being scared, the monster movie genre will never die.

MYTHICAL MONSTERS

The Golem

— 1915–1920 —

The 1915 silent horror film, *The Golem*, directed by Paul Wegener, is generally regarded as the first ever monster movie. The plot was inspired by an ancient legend from Jewish folklore. According to the original story, a 16th century Rabbi, named Judah Loew ben Bezalel, created a magical creature to protect the ghetto in Prague from anti-Semitic attacks. He constructed the golem from clay from the banks of the Vltava river, and brought it to life using magic and Hebrew incantations. Unfortunately, the Rabbi lost control of the golem and it became increasingly violent, prompting the Rabbi to find a way to stop it.

The first film in Paul Wegener's series is set in the early 20th century. The plot centres on the story of an antiques dealer, played by Henrik Galeen, who finds a golem, played by Paul Wegener. The dealer resurrects the golem to use him as a servant, but the golem falls in love with the dealer's wife. She does not return his affections, so, broken hearted, the golem embarks on a series of murders.

The Golem was followed by two further films; *The Golem and The Dancing Girl* (1917) and *The Golem: How He Came into the World* (1920). The first sequel has a comedic edge and features Paul Wegener donning the golem's make-up in order to frighten a girl he's infatuated with. Like its 1915 predecessor, it is now classified as a lost film. The third film, which follows more closely the original legend, has survived and is now the best known of the three. It is widely regarded as a horror masterpiece.

The Sinbad Trilogy

RICH MAN, POOR MAN

The ancient tales of Sinbad the Sailor are like those of *1001 Nights*, or Chaucer's *Canterbury Tales*, in that they exist within a frame story. Sinbad's particular frame story goes as follows:

In the days of Haroun al-Rashid, Caliph of Baghdad (766–809), a poor man, whose job it was to carry goods around the town, sits to rest on a bench outside the house of a rich merchant. Tired and depressed, he complains aloud to Allah about the unfairness of a world in which the rich live a life of ease, whilst the poor toil endlessly and yet remain poor. The rich merchant hears him and invites him in. Discovering that they are both named Sinbad, he begins to tell him the story of the seven voyages he took in order to secure his riches — these are the Seven Voyages of Sinbad the Sailor.

THE 7TH VOYAGE OF SINBAD

— 1958 —

The first film in the Sinbad trilogy may be named *The 7th Voyage of Sinbad*, but this is misleading, as it bares little relation to the original story of the 7th voyage. The plot actually has more in common with the second and the third voyages from the original tales, and the monsters featured in the film, the Cyclops and the Roc bird, are taken from these stories.

WIZARD'S LAMP

In this film, Sinbad, played by Kerwin Mathews, is on his way to Baghdad with his wife to be, the Princess Parisa, played by Kathryn Grant. They stop at the isle of Colossa to collect provisions, but while they are there, Sinbad's crew are attacked by a giant, fearsome one-eyed Cyclops. Their lives are saved by a mysterious wizard called Sokurah, played by Torin Thatcher, but, in saving the crew, Sokurah loses his magic lamp to the Cyclops, and asks Sinbad to return to Colossa to win it back. Sinbad refuses, and so Sokurah casts an evil spell on Parisa, shrinking her to roughly the size of Sinbad's palm. The only way for Sinbad to break the spell, and marry his beloved, is to return to Colossa and find the egg of the giant Roc bird.

STOP-MOTION ANIMATION

The 7th Voyage of Sinbad was the first film ever to feature Ray Harryhausen's 'Dynamation' technique — his particular brand of stop-motion model animation. Harryhausen was a huge fan of Willis O'Brien, the legendary special effects man whose work can be seen in such monster movie classics as *The Lost World* and *King Kong*. He even got a job as O'Brien's assistant in order to learn everything he possibly could from his idol. In fact, Harryhausen's career owes a lot to O'Brien. The 1952 re-release of *King Kong* sparked a renewed public interest in big monster movies, and this renewed interest must have helped to get the Sinbad films made.

The animation sequences in *The 7th Voyage of Sinbad* were so extensive that it took 11 months for him to complete them. In isolation, the fight sequence between the dragon

Cyclops and the dragon. Scene from *The 7th Voyage of Sinbad* (1958).

and the Cyclops took two to three weeks of his time. The Cyclops was based, in part, on images of the Greek God, Pan. It has a large horn in the centre of its head, hoofed feet and furry legs like a satyr. Other elements of its appearance resemble Ymir from 20 *Million Miles to Earth* — another of Harryhausen's legendary characters — in that it is covered in scales and has spiked spinal ridges running down its back, its arms and three-pronged claws are also very similar.

....

SNAKEWOMAN

The Cyclops might have proven popular with cinema audiences, and fans of the genre, but, as monsters go, Harryhausen's personal favourite was the snakewoman, who plays little or no part in the story but is created by the wizard Sokurah in order to entertain the court of the Caliph of Baghdad. She was inspired by a belly dancer that Harryhausen saw perform in Beruit, and bares a passing resemblance to the Hindu Goddess Kali, who makes an appearance in *The Golden Voyage of Sinbad* (1973).

Apart from the Cyclops, the other major monster in the movie is the Roc bird; a giant two-headed eagle-like creature that attacks the crew after hunger forces them to kill and cook its chick. It's an impressive piece of animation but the Roc doesn't convey any of the character, or give the 'performance' that made Cyclops so popular. Other creatures Harryhausen created for the film included a dragon and a skeleton swordsman, the latter of which proved so popular with moviegoers that Harryhausen eventually returned to and expanded upon it, creating a whole legion of skeletal soldiers for *Jason and the Argonauts* (1963). The idea of a skeleton army has also permeated other films, most notably those of the recent *The Pirates of the Caribbean* franchise.

THE GOLDEN VOYAGE OF SINBAD
— 1973 —

The Golden Voyage of Sinbad is the second of three Sinbad films produced by Ray Harryhausen and Charles H. Schneer. This one stars John Phillip Law as Sinbad and features a range of mythically inspired animated monsters including a homunculus, a one-eyed centaur, a griffin and the Goddess Kali. The film was shot for a relatively miniscule budget of $982,351. Despite this, it managed to win the first ever Saturn award for Best Fantasy Film, an accolade later shared by such enormous productions as *The Lord of the Rings* trilogy (2001–2003) and *The Curious Case of Benjamin Button* (2008).

SINBAD AND THE EYE OF THE TIGER
— 1977 —

The third and final Sinbad film that Harryhausen and Schneer made for Columbia, stars Patrick Wayne in the role of Sinbad and Jane Seymour as Princess Farah, his amour. The mythical monsters don't come as thick and fast in this movie as in the other two, but there are some notable appearances; a golden creature named Minoton — a golem/Minotaur hybrid — is perhaps the most fantastical. He is brought to life by the evil witch, Queen Zenobia, as are three ghouls, or zomboids, who attempt to pick off members of Sinbad's crew. Perhaps surprisingly, the ghouls, who were referred to as 'nightmare creatures' in the storyboard, bare no resemblance to the popular notion of what a zombie or a ghoul should look like; they are much more insect-like, with skeletal bodies, enormous bug-like eyes and antennae.

'Release the Kraken!' Scene from *Clash of the Titans* (1981).

Jason and the Argonauts
— 1963 —

Jason and the Argonauts has been called the *Gone With The Wind* of stop-frame animation. Many regard it as Ray Harryhausen's best work and it is awash with mythical monsters, including Talos, the man of bronze; Medusa, a trio of harpies; many-headed dragons as well as a legion of skeleton soldiers. In April 2004, *Empire* magazine ranked Talos the second best movie monster of all time, behind King Kong, who was the brainchild of Harryhausen's idol, Willis O'Brien.

Clash of the Titans
— 1981 —

The original *Clash of the Titans* has become known as a cult classic by fantasy film buffs and children of the 1980s. It stars Laurence Olivier, Harry Hamlin, Judi Bowker, Ursula Andress and Maggie Smith. The plot is based on the myth of the Greek hero, Perseus, but it includes numerous deviations from the original tale. Ray Harryhausen, who co-produced the film, used stop-motion animation to create the movie's monsters, which include the Kraken and the gorgon, Medusa. He retired from film-making shortly after *Clash of the Titans*, making this his last full-length feature film.

A 3D remake of *Clash of the Titans* was released in 2010 by Warner Bros. It is an affectionate homage to the original film, but the plot is only loosely based on the Greek myth. It stars Liam Neeson, in Laurence Olivier's role as Zeus, Ralph Fiennes as the evil Hades and Gemma Arterton as Io, a woman who has been rendered ageless as a punishment from the gods. The film came in for some heavy criticism from a wide variety of sources. In general, people did not approve of the decision to bolt on 3D. Perhaps if this film had been made in isolation, without the 1981 classic casting a shadow over it, the film might have been better received.

Pan's Labyrinth
— 2006 —

Directed by the Academy Award-winning Mexican, Guillermo del Toro, *Pan's Labyrinth* is set in rural Spain in 1944, towards the end of the civil war. A young girl named Ofélia moves with her recently remarried mother and unborn brother to the home of her new step-father, Vidal, an authoritarian captain in Franco's army. Unhappy with her new life, and frightened of her mother's new husband, she finds refuge in the old abandoned labyrinth she discovers next to the family house. There she meets Faun, a magical guardian who suspects her to be the long lost princess of the underworld. But, in order to claim her title and earn her freedom she must perform three dangerous tasks.

Del Toro's monsters are heavily influenced by myth, folklore and fairytale. Probably the most frightening of them all is Pale Man, a large, grotesque, child-eating monster with eyes in the palms of his hands. He sits mo-tionless and silent at a feast-laden table in the heart of the labyrinth. Ofélia is warned not to eat anything from the table, but she is unable to resist, and steals two grapes. Pale Man awakes, and fiercely pursues her, eating two of her fairy companions during the chase. Del Toro has referred to the story as a parable. He calls it a spiritual sequel to his earlier film, *The Devil's Backbone*, a gothic thriller also set in Spain during the same time period.

The incredible monsters in *Pan's Labyrinth* were brought to life using actors in make-up (del Toro is an ex make-up supervisor), animatronics and CGI (computer generated imagery) technology. Doug Jones, the actor who played Faun and Pale Man, had already worked with del Toro on *Mimic* (1997) and *Hellboy* (2004). Del Toro reputedly sent the actor an email telling him he was the only person who could play those parts, despite the fact that Jones spoke no Spanish — the film's language. Jones apparently learned the lines phonetically, before a Spanish actor overdubbed them.

The Pale Man, the grotesque monster from *Pan's Labyrinth* (2006).

HUMANOIDS

Nosferatu

A SYMPHONY OF HORROR
— 1922 —

Nosferatu is a classic horror film of the German Expressionist tradition. Made in 1922 and directed by F. W. Murnau, it was the one and only production of Prana Film, a company founded in 1921 by producers Enrico Dieckmann and Albin Grau. Grau was inspired to make a vampire film following an experience he had during World War I. At some point during the winter of 1916, a Serbian farmer told Grau that his father was a vampire, and one of the undead.

Dieckmann and Grau asked Henrik Galeen to write a screenplay based on Bram Stoker's classic novel *Dracula* (1897), but they failed to obtain the film rights, so all the names had to be changed, as did some of the plot details. Galeen had previously worked with Paul Wegener on the *Golem* trilogy and was gaining a reputation as something of a specialist in the genre.

SILENCE IS FRIGHTENING

The character of Nosferatu differs from other celluloid vampires in that he lacks the kind of sexual allure we've come to associate with later incarnations of the vampire. Nosferatu is quite hideous to look at and bat-like, with pointed ears, dark, deep-set eyes, sharp teeth and long, tapering fingernails. This is usually attributed to the fact that *Nosferatu* was a silent film. The film-makers required Orlock to appear gruesome in order to convey his scariness without sound. Nosferatu also kills his victims rather than transforming them into fellow vampires. He must sleep by day, because exposure to sunlight could kill him, whereas Dracula is only weakened by sunlight. *Nosferatu*'s ending also differs substantially from that of Bram Stoker's novel.

THE VAMPYRE
— 1979 —

The 1979 version of the film, *Nosferatu the Vampyre*, is a reworking of the original. It portrays Orlock, now named Dracula, as the same creepy looking rodent-like creature. It stars Klaus Kinski a popular actor who had worked with the director, Werner Herzog, on several other films, as Count Dracula. The year 1979 saw a vampire movie revival that included films such as the lavish *Dracula* remake with Frank Langella, *Nightwing* and the spoof, *Love at First Bite*. Even the children's TV show *Sesame Street* had a Count von Count, but he had much more in common with Bela Lugosi, than with Klaus Kinski. He also debuted years earlier, making his first appearance in 1972.

The Phantom of the Opera

SILENT FILM
— 1925 —

The Phantom of the Opera was first made as a silent film in 1925. An adaptation of the novel by Gaston Leroux, it was directed by Rupert Julian and starred Lon Chaney as the masked phantom. After initial screenings the studio, Universal, was unhappy with the film's quality and so brought in other directors to reshoot and re-edit large portions of the film. When the finished version finally hit movie theatres it proved a financial and critical success. It was *Phantom* that inspired Universal to commission a whole host of other horror classics including *Dracula* (1931), *Frankenstein* (1931) and *The Wolf Man* (1941).

••••

MONSTROUS MAKE-UP

The 1925 version of *Phantom* is most famous for Chaney's monstrous make-up, which he applied himself, and was kept a studio secret until the first showing. Chaney made a habit of doing his own gruesome make-up after the success of *The Hunchback of Notre Dame* in 1923, in which he also starred. For *Phantom*, Chaney set out to achieve a skull-like appearance. He painted his eye sockets black and pulled the tip of his nose up, pinning it in place with wire. He enlarged his nostrils using black paint and used a set of jagged false teeth to complete the look. The effect is pretty arresting even by today's standards. The scene in which the heroine, Christine, unmasks her captor, revealing his deformed features, apparently caused moviegoers to scream and faint in the aisles when the film was first shown.

Of all the film and stage versions of *Phantom*, this film sticks most closely to Leroux's original vision for the Phantom. In subsequent versions it is claimed that he was hideously disfigured in an accident at the Opera House, but here, as in the novel, he was born with his deformity. It is unclear why this aspect of the story has been altered over time, but one imagines it has something to do with our changing attitudes towards disability and disfigurement. Crucially though, the ending of the 1925 film differs significantly from the ending in the novel. Leroux intended that the Phantom should die alone, of a broken heart, in the bowels of

the Opera House. Originally, the film shared the book's ending, but preview audiences didn't like it, so they changed the story to accommodate a more dramatic conclusion.

••••••••••••••••••••••••••

STAGE AND SCREEN
— 2004 —

The well-known 2004 film adaptation of *Phantom of the Opera* is based on Andrew Lloyd Webber's 1986 musical of the same name, which, in turn, is based on Leroux's novel. Plans to make a film version of the hit musical first arose as early as 1989. Lloyd Webber originally wanted to cast the stars of the stage version, Sarah Brightman and Michael Crawford, in the lead roles, but his divorce from Sarah Brightman made this impossible. This, coupled with director, Joel Schumacher's busy schedule, meant that the whole concept had to be put on ice for a number of years. By the time they got round to recasting and actually shooting the movie, the budget had swelled from $25 million to $70 million. Advances in technology meant that they could achieve much more in terms of the look of the film, but in turn, audience expectations had risen. The 2004 version of *Phantom* made a healthy profit at the box office, but received mixed reviews from critics, who complimented the films look, but were less than impressed by the script and the actors' performances.

Dracula
••••••••••••••••••••••••••

LUGOSI'S COUNT
— 1931 —

The name Bela Lugosi has become synonymous with the character of Count Dracula thanks to his role in the 1931 film of the same name. Unlike earlier adaptations of Bram

'I am Dracula' - Bela Lugosi as the Count in *Dracula* (1931).

Stoker's classic novel, this film had the benefit of sound, and so could rely on Lugosi's thick Hungarian accent for dramatic effect. Lugosi was therefore free to become a better-looking, more seductive vampire; he had no need of the heavy make-up worn by Maz Schreck in *Nosferatu*. In fact, Lugosi didn't even wear fangs in his portrayal of the Count.

Interestingly, Lugosi was not the producer, Carl Laemmle Jr's first choice for the role of Count Dracula. That accolade goes to Lon Chaney, who had already starred in such monstrous films as *The Hunchback of Notre Dame* (1923) and *The Phantom of the Opera* (1925). This would imply that the makers were originally looking for a heavily made-up ghoulish vampire, rather than the dashing and debonair figure cut by Lugosi. Unfortunately, Chaney succumbed to cancer before the casting process began, and the onset of the Great Depression in the US meant that the film-makers had to widen their search to include less expensive, unknown actors. Lugosi lobbied the film's executives, and eventually won them over by agreeing to accept a very low wage. *Dracula*'s director, Tod Browning, was apparently so disenchanted at losing his intended leading man that he lost all interest in the making of the film and left a lot of the work to his assistant. With audiences, though, Lugosi's performance was an instant hit.

Lugosi died in 1956 following a heart attack and was buried wearing one of his famous Dracula capes. When the actors Vincent Price and Peter Lorre went to view Lugosi's body, Lorre quipped 'do you think we should drive a stake through his heart, just in case?'

HAMMER HORROR
— 1958 —

In the course of his career, Christopher Lee has played the Prince of Darkness in no less than nine films, beginning in 1958 with Hammer Horror's *Dracula*, known in the US as *Horror of Dracula*.

The plot of this film differs in a number of ways from Bram Stoker's novel. Firstly, and perhaps most confusingly, Jonathan Harker is engaged to be married to Lucy Holmwood, and Mina is the name of Arthur Holmwood's wife. Consequently Lucy is the object of Dracula's desire, not Mina. Secondly, Jonathan Harker is not a solicitor, but a librarian who arrives at Dracula's castle in order to help organize the Count's library (his true mission is, in fact, to kill Dracula, although it is not clear who sent him). This means that there is no property deal, and the Count never comes to England, all of the film's action takes place in Transylvania. In this version of the story Dracula only uses two magical powers. He can hypnotize women with his eyes, and he can travel through fog. He does not transform into a bat, and he only has one vampire bride rather than the original three. Like Count Orlock in *Nosferatu*, Lee's Dracula can be killed by sunlight. In Stoker's original, the Count is simply weakened by the power of the sun.

CHANNELLING LUGOSI

Appearance wise, all Lugosi's trademarks have been taken and amplified; the widow's peak is more pronounced, as is his pallor. His fangs drip blood and the whites of his eyes are stained red. Interestingly, legend has it that whenever he played Dracula, Lee wore a ring that had once belonged to Bela Lugosi. Replicas of this ring are available for purchase on various collectibles websites, pictures of which appear to show an ancient family crest engraved in a carnelian stone. Lee remains a huge fan of the horror genre and continues to embrace the cult following it has given him.

BRAM STOKER'S DRACULA
— 1992 —

The Hollywood actress, Winona Ryder, brought James V. Hart's script for a TV movie called *Dracula, the Untold Story* to the attention of director Francis Ford Coppola as a peace offering, after the two fell out during the making of *The Godfather III*, when Ryder pulled out of her role in the late stages, delaying production. Coppola, an avid fan of Bram Stoker's novel, enjoyed the sensual elements of the screenplay and wanted to create a visually rich and luxurious film version that resembled an 'erotic dream'.

. . . .

DREAM CAST

Coppola invested a large chunk of the movie's budget in costume, in order to showcase what he thought was the film's best asset — its cast. It included Keanu Reeves as Jonathan Harker, Winona Ryder as Mina Harker, Gary Oldman as the Count and Anthony Hopkins as Van Helsing. Given Coppola's reputation for delivering his movies late, he was determined to deliver this one on time and on budget. This led to the use of sound stages to avoid trouble caused by filming outside in inclement weather.

Gary Oldman's portrayal of Count Dracula brings him up-to-date somewhat. His bears little resemblance to Bela Lugosi's unforgettable portrayal of the Prince of Darkness. Where Lugosi played the Count as evil through and through, Oldman sought to play him as a fallen angel, a warrior who rejects Christianity and turns to the powers of the underworld when he learns of his beloved wife, Elizabeta's suicide. When he sees a picture of Mina Harker, Dracula becomes convinced that she is a reincarnated version of his late wife, and vows to do whatever it takes in order to spend eternity in her embrace.

Coppola's version of the legend was generally well-received and turned a profit at the box office, but some critics regarded it as over blown, over long and over complicated. Oldman's character appears on screen in numerous forms including Vlad Drac himself, a young nobleman, a plague of rats, a rampaging werewolf and a disembodied pair of eyes. The addition of a love story between Dracula and Mina Harker also muddies the waters a little. Some regard it as an innovative attempt to bring some hopeful message to the story, others seem to think it further complicates an already intricate plot.

Frankenstein

A CHILLING THRILLER
— 1931 —

The first film version of *Frankenstein*, based on Peggy Webling's stage adaptation of Mary Shelley's novel, is regarded by many as one of the greatest films of all time. John L. Balderston was charged with taking Webling's play and further adapting it for Universal Studios, despite the fact that he was not at all keen on Webling's original work, branding it 'illiterate' and 'inconceivably crude'.

Like Webling's play, the film's plot is very different from that of the book. The film seems to conclude that the source of the monster's wrongdoing is its possession of a 'criminal brain', which determines his violent actions. In the book, Shelley paints a picture of a basically innocent creature who turns evil as a result of society's ill treatment of him.

It is this 1931 film version of Mary Shelley's story that has largely defined the iconic image of Frankenstein's monster. The angular shaped head, mono-brow and the bolted neck are all features of Boris Karloff's celluloid monster. They were not born of the book. Jack Pierce was the make-up artist who designed the monster's flattened head. The inspiration for its look was originally based on Paul Wegener's character Golem, from the film of the same name, since studio head Carl Laemmle Jr and the original director, Robert Florey, were both extremely familiar with the German Expressionist genre of films. But, when James Whale replaced Florey as director, and Boris Karloff replaced Bela Lugosi in the lead role, Pierce came up with a look that reinforced the monster's back-story. Hence, the monster's head bears a scar where Dr Frankenstein has accessed the brain cavity. The bolts on the monster's neck are actually electrodes used to carry the electricity generated by the lightning strike into the monster's body. Incidentally, a double had to stand in for the famous 'birth' scene in which lightning strikes the monster's body, because Karloff was terrified of being electrocuted by the live voltage on the stage. Kenneth Strickfaden designed the electrical effects, and apparently even managed to source a Tesla coil built by Nikola Tesla himself.

Jack Pierce was known to be an extremely stern man, but his relationship with Karloff was a good one. His relationship with Lon Chaney, however, couldn't have been more different. The two despised one another and were constantly at each other's throats. They worked together on a number of Universal's iconic horror movies, including *The Mummy* and *The Wolf Man* franchises. But both men could be very stubborn and difficult to work with, and the make-ups involved a lot of time, energy and in some cases, physical discomfort and pain. It was a recipe for disharmony between cast and crew. Pierce's personal reputation may not have been that great, but his work has stood the test of time.

Amongst all the make-ups he devised during his movie career, Frankenstein's monster is as instantly recognizable as it is timeless.

IT'S ALIVE!
— 1994 —

The star-studded cast of the film version, *Mary Shelly's Frankenstein*, includes Robert De Niro in the role of the monster, Helena Bonham Carter as Elizabeth and Kenneth Branagh as Dr Frankenstein. Branagh also directed the movie. As indicated by the title, compared with the 1931 version, the plot follows more closely that of Shelley's novel. De Niro's monster is horribly disfigured and scarred, but looks very different from Boris Karloff's portrayal of the monster. Gone is the flat head, the mono-brow and the electrodes. Like the monster in the book, De Niro's monster has a round head, and scarred, decaying skin.

Despite its amazing cast and substantial budget, the film was not particularly well received by critics. De Niro's performance as the monster went down quite well but most people regarded this as an overly ambitious attempt by Branagh. It certainly has not proved as unforgettable as the 1931 film which is over 60 years older, and yet springs immediately to mind whenever the words 'horror' and 'classic' are mentioned in the same sentence.

The Mummy

IT COMES TO LIFE!
— 1932 —

Directed by Karl Freund, the 1932 version of *The Mummy* is set in 1921, when an expeditionary team discovers the tomb of an ancient Egyptian named Imhotep, who was buried alive as punishment for attempting to bring his dead beloved back to life. Also in the tomb is the 'Scroll of Thoth', a magical text which, if read aloud, has the power to resurrect the dead. One of the younger members of the team reads the spell aloud, awakening the 3,700 year-old mummy. Imhotep escapes to Cairo only to appear again 10 years later, disguised as a modern-day Egyptian hell-bent on finding the woman he believes to be the reincarnation of his ancient love.

The Mummy is another one of those classic Universal horror movies of the 1930s. It stars Boris Karloff, of *Frankenstein* fame, in the role of Imhotep, the revived Egyptian priest. Alongside Karloff are Zita Johann as Helen Grosvenor, David Manners as Frank Whemple and Edward Van Sloan as Dr Muller.

....

TUTANKHAMEN'S TOMB

The film was inspired by the discovery of Tutankhamen's tomb in 1922. Studio boss Carl Laemmle Jr asked Richard Shayer to find a literary source for an Egypt-themed horror movie. Richard Shayer was unable to find anything suitable, but the plot of *The Mummy* does seem to be based loosely on a short story by Edgar Allen Poe entitled *The Ring of Thoth*. In true Universal tradition, the make-up for *The Mummy* was devised by Jack Pierce, who based his design on pictures he had seen of Seti II. It took around nine hours for Pierce to transform Karloff into Imhotep, which is why he is only in full make-up for a few of the movie's scenes, in the rest, he is wearing a scaled-down version. Karloff is said to have found the make-up process highly uncomfortable. He called it 'the most trying ordeal I have ever endured.' For all Karloff's suffering, the finished effect is undoubtedly worth it.

UNIVERSAL STUDIOS
— 1999 —

The year 1999 saw Universal Studios take another look at their classic collection of horror movies of the 1930s, with the aim of making some much needed cash. The plot of this remake differs slightly from the original. It centres on the characters of Rick O'Connell (Brendan Fraser), Evelyn Carnahan (Rachel Weisz) and Jon Carnahan (John Hannah) as they set out on an expedition to unearth (amongst other things) the book of Amun-Ra, a solid gold book capable of taking life away. When they finally arrive in Hamunaptra, they discover the mummy of Imhotep instead.

The Invisible Man
— 1933 —

Based on the 1897 science fiction novel by H.G. Wells, *The Invisible Man* was adapted for screen by R. C. Sherriff, Philip Wylie and Preston Sturges, although Sturges's work was deemed unsatisfactory, and he was taken off the project. The plot centres on a scientist named Jack Griffin, who discovers a drug called Monocaine, which can render his entire body invisible to the naked eye. Unfortunately, it also makes him murderously insane. In this, the film differs from the book as Wells' original protagonist was mad to begin with, and deliberately made himself invisible in order to commit crime. In the film, it is simply an effect of the drug — and when the drug wears off, so does Griffin's malevolence.

....

ACTIONS SPEAK LOUDER THAN WORDS?

The English actor Claude Rains takes the title role in *The Invisible Man*, although,

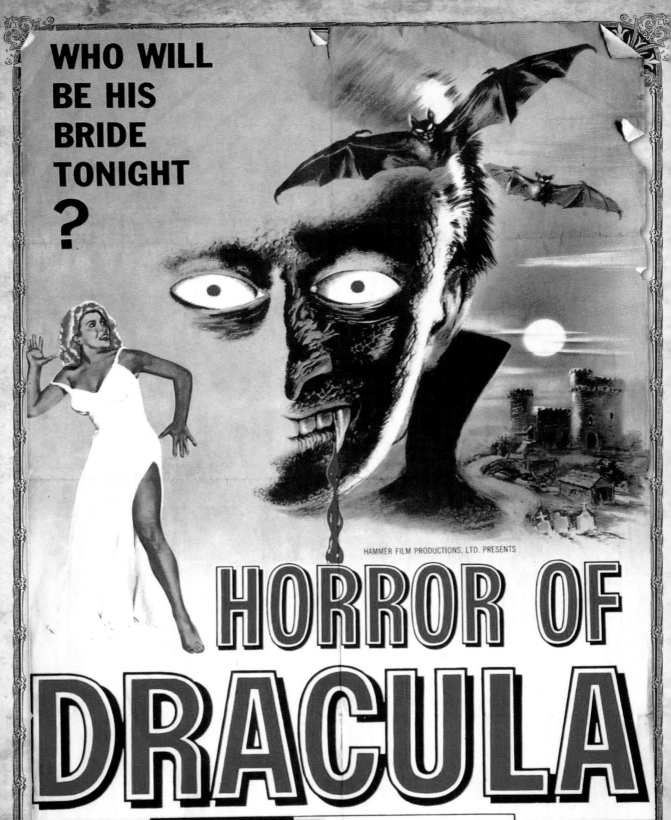

WHO WILL BE HIS BRIDE TONIGHT?

HAMMER FILM PRODUCTIONS, LTD. PRESENTS

HORROR OF DRACULA

Brilliant **TECHNICOLOR!**

...SA STRIBLING with CHRISTOPHER LEE as DRACULA

Executive producer · Associate producer · Produced by
...ICHAEL CARRERAS · ANTHONY NELSON-KEYS · ANTHONY HINDS

...RNA...NAL RELEASE

A 1958 movie poster for *Horror of Dracula* released as *Dracula* in Europe. Hammer's famous film was the first Dracula movie to incorporate fangs, blood, and red eyes and brings arguably the best Dracula to the screen – Christopher Lee. Lee said the fangs he wore were easy to speak with, but not to eat with. The contact lenses he wore were very painful and made his vision blurred.

A movie poster for the classic Universal Pictures *The Invisible Man* (1933) directed by James Whale and starring Claude Rains. A scientist turns himself invisible. However, the formula slowly drives him insane, causing him to terrorize the countryside as an invisible killer. Curiously enough, although the Invisible Man has to be naked to be invisible, the footprints he leaves in the snow at the end of the film are those of a man wearing shoes.

for the bulk of the film only his voice appears. It is not until the very end of the film that we actually see him. Rains was not the studio's first choice for the part of Griffin. They wanted Boris Karloff, but he backed out after Carl Laemmle Jr tried one too many times to lower his contractual wage. Rains came on board because the director, James Whale, liked the 'intellectual' sound of his voice. As a result of his appearance in this film, Rains' career took off. He later appeared in classic Hollywood blockbusters such as *The Adventures of Robin Hood* (1938), *Mr. Smith Goes to Washington* (1939), *The Wolf Man* (1941) and *Casablanca* (1942).

. . . .

SPECIAL EFFECTS

The Invisible Man uses groundbreaking special effects, which were developed especially for the film. Three men were responsible for these; John P. Fulton, John J. Mescall and Frank D. Williams and, as a result, they usually get the credit for the film's success. The movements of a naked Invisible Man could be recreated using wires, but the effect of a partially clothed Invisible Man was not so easily done. This was achieved by dressing Rains in an all-in-on black velvet suit, and filming him against a black velvet background. The shot was then combined with a shot of the location where the scene took place, using a matte process. Rains suffered from claustrophobia and found the filming of these scenes so unpleasant that, often, a double had to be used. In 2009, the film was selected by the United States National Film Registry and the Library of Congress as being 'culturally, historically or aesthetically significant'. *The Invisible Man* was subsequently built upon, remade and parodied, but none of the later films, or TV series' were anything like as well-received as the original.

The Wolf Man

. . . .

LON CHANEY JR
– 1941 –

The Wolf Man, starring Lon Chaney Jr, is the last of the classic monster movies made by Universal Pictures, coming a whole decade after Bela Lugosi's *Dracula* (1931) became a box office sensation. Larry Talbot is the second son of a British lord, who returns to the Welsh village of his birth when his older brother is killed in a mysterious hunting accident. Larry falls in love with a local girl, Gwen Conliffe (played by Evelyn Ankers), but, when a mutual friend is attacked by a werewolf his efforts at saving her life result in him being bitten by the beast. Doomed to become a werewolf himself, Larry struggles against the urge to kill those closest to him. That is until, finally, the urge becomes too much.

. . . .

CENSORED

By today's standards Lon Chaney's performance in the lead role remains strong, but the wolf man's appearance is less than convincing. When you realize that the make-up supervisor, Jack Pierce, was working with primitive materials like glue, cotton and yak hair, it's hardly surprising. Interestingly, censors of the time actively prevented the character from looking too scary, and would not allow a direct man to beast transformation. This worked out well for Universal, it meant they saved the big metamorphosis scene for the film's climax. *The Wolf Man* proved popular with critics and moviegoers, and, although the character never starred in another feature, he did appear alongside other Universal monsters in numerous other films – such as *Frankenstein meets the Wolf Man* (1943), *The House of Dracula* (1945) and *Abbott and Costello Meet Frankenstein* (1948).

with

Claude RAINS   Warren WILLIAM

Ralph BELLAMY   Patric KNOWLES

Bela LUGOSI   Maria OUSPENSKAYA
Evelyn ANKERS

and Lon CHANEY

Directed by GEORGE WAGGNER
Associate Producer GEORGE WAGGNER
A UNIVERSAL PICTURE

BENICIO DEL TORO

— 2010 —

The Wolfman is a remake of the 1941 classic, starring Benicio del Toro in the role of Lawrence Talbot (previously played by Lon Chaney Jr). Supporting cast members include Anthony Hopkins as Lawrence's father Sir John Talbot and Emily Blunt as Gwen Conliffe, who in this instance, is the fiancée of Lawrence's dead brother. The second half of this film differs significantly from the original and the ending involves a major twist that the 1941 version does not. The film's theatrical release was greeted with mostly unfavourable reviews, but as time has gone on the movie seems to have garnered more appreciation and has enjoyed greater success on DVD than at the cinema.

Hulk

ERIC BANA IS HULK

— 2003 —

The Incredible Hulk began as an American TV series between 1978—1982, based on the Marvel comic book character of the same name, which was created by Stan Lee and Jack Kirby. The 2003 film was directed by Ang Lee and written by James Shamus, Michael France and John Turman. It starred

The Wolf Man was released in 1941 by Universal Pictures. Directed by George Waggner and starred Lon Chaney Jr.

Eric Bana as Dr Bruce Banner, a scientist who is doomed to transform into a vengeful monster whenever he gets angry.

Hulk focusses on the origins of the story, and the plot bares some resemblance to another Universal monster flick: *Wolf Man*, in that it concentrates on a violent power struggle between an estranged father and son. There is even a character named Major Talbot, a clear reference to the *Wolf Man* films. It is not clear where the inspiration for this reference came from though, because the film spent so long in the early stages of development. Development began as early as 1990, a whole 13 years prior to the eventual release, but Universal couldn't decide exactly what kind of movie they wanted. In the end so many different versions of the script were written, by so many different people, that it's no longer easy to see which idea came from which original source.

····

PSYCHODRAMA

Ang Lee set out to make a tragedy and psychodrama, in which the Hulk embodies the green monster of rage, jealousy, greed and fear in all of us. It turns out that Bruce Banner's childhood was an intensely traumatic and abusive one, and it is this early trauma that the Hulk draws upon — not exactly the standard premise for a movie that was rated 12A in the UK but, then again lots of classic family-friendly films manage to tackle bigger, more serious issues of a similar nature. Eric Bana went on record as saying that he found the shoot 'Ridiculously serious…a silent set, morbid in lots of ways'. As part of his preparation for the role, Lee took Bana to see a bare-knuckle boxing fight.

When *Hulk* was released in theatres the critics' reviews were mixed, one major criticism was that, at 138 minutes, it's far too long. In its opening weekend the movie did well,

but they dropped off quickly and overall box office takings were not reassuring. The film became the largest opener not to earn upwards of $150 million in North America.

· ·

ED NORTON IS INCREDIBLE
— 2008 —

Compared to Ang Lee's 2003 version of the Hulk, the 2008 reboot, directed by Louis Leterrier, is a completely different animal. For starters, the Hulk's back-story differs dramatically. In this movie Bruce Banner, played by Ed Norton, is exposed to gamma radiation as part of an experiment to create a regenerating super soldier. The experiment goes wrong and Bruce transforms into the Hulk, destroys the laboratory, injures his girlfriend, research scientist Betty, and goes on the run, becoming a fugitive from the United States Army.

David Duchovny, of X-files fame, was the studio's first choice to play Bruce, but Norton hooked the role when one of the film's producers, Gale Anne Hurd, recalled Norton's portrayals of schizoid characters in *Primal Fear* (1996) and *Fight Club* (1999). Norton was also noted as possessing a similar frame and personality to Bill Bixby, who played Bruce in the original TV series. Norton was a massive fan of *The Incredible Hulk* and had expressed an interest in the part when the original movie was cast. He also rewrote the script, an effort which, according to Leterrier, added real gravitas to the story.

Ultimately this 2008 reboot fared better at the box office than its 2003 predecessor. It slightly out-grossed its older cousin and received much better reviews. In general, critics were relieved to see a return to good old-fashioned super-hero movie-making after Ang Lee's version went so off message.

DINOSAURS, GIANT LIZARDS AND OVERSIZED ANIMALS

The Lost World
— 1925 —

The Lost World is the silent movie adaptation of Arthur Conan Doyle's 1912 novel of the same name. This is the first dinosaur-based celluloid hit and, as such, every other monster movie of this kind, from *King Kong* to *Jurassic Park*, stems from it. It was the first feature-length movie ever to include model animation as a major special effect and possibly the first to use stop-motion animation in general. In 1998, the Library of Congress selected it for preservation in the United States National Film Registry.

The movie's plot tells the story of Paula White, the daughter of an explorer named Maple White, who has gone missing some-

Scene from *The Lost World* (1925). The first film adaptation of Sir Arthur Conan Doyle's classic novel about a land where prehistoric creatures still roam.

where in the Amazon. One day Paula arrives at the office of the eccentric Professor Challenger clutching her father's diary, which, she claims, proves the continued existence of living dinosaurs. Professor Challenger announces this fact to the academic community, who dismiss his claims as lunacy. Determined to prove them all wrong, the Professor and Paula assemble a team that includes a well-known big game hunter named Sir John Roxton and a newspaper journalist called Ed Malone. Together they set off to rescue Maple White and track down the dinosaurs described in his journal.

When they arrive at the place where Maple White was last seen, it quickly becomes clear that there is indeed prehistoric life at large in the jungle. Now they must find out what has become of him, and bring back some evidence that his claims were real. But, before they do any of that, they need to escape the lost world alive.

····

DINOSAURS OF THE 1920S

Whilst showcasing film-making methods of the day, *The Lost World* also tells us a lot about what people of the 1920s believed about dinosaurs. For a start, the existence of a few of the creatures featured in the film has since been written off by palaeontologists, and many more were completely different from how they are depicted here. Still, Arthur Conan Doyle was so impressed by the groundbreaking animation sequences that he showed it at a dinner for the American Society of Magicians, for a group of respected magicians including his good friend, Harry Houdini. It's not clear whether he meant it as an entertaining trick, or if he really set out to convince them that the images showed genuine dinosaurs, but he refused to tell them exactly where the footage had come from, or to succumb to any question-

ing on the matter. In fact, the animation sequences were created by the pioneering special effects master Willis O'Brien, but the magicians were utterly mystified by what they saw, and the stunt served as valuable PR for the film. Overnight Conan Doyle had managed to make it the most highly anticipated movie in America.

King Kong

THE ICONIC ORIGINAL
— 1933 —

King Kong is perhaps the most iconic monster movie ever made. Kong's image has transcended the famous film franchise and can now be found on everything from product packaging to political propaganda. The original story was conceived and created by the film-maker Merian C. Cooper, who had been fascinated by gorillas since reading *Explorations and Adventures in Equatorial Africa*, by Paul Du Chaillu. The idea of a giant ape-like creature lusting after a human woman was nothing new, in 1887, Emmanuel Frémiet depicted an extremely Kong-like scene in his sculpture entitled *Gorille enlevant une femme*, or *Gorilla Carrying Off A Woman*. Cooper seems to have been more motivated by his interest in gorillas, than by any potential relationship between gorillas and humans. Fay Wray's character and the kidnap scenario were both added at a fairly late stage in the development process, when the studio complained that Cooper's treatment lacked romance. As a result the movie's plot wound up looking like this:

It's the year 1933, and Carl Denham, a film director and explorer (played by Robert Armstrong) needs to finish shooting a film starring Ann Darrow, a beautiful young starlet (famously played by Fay Wray). They sail to the mysterious Skull Island, where Ann is kidnapped by natives and prepared as a sacrifice to their gorilla god – Kong. Kong discovers Ann tied to an altar near his lair and falls instantly in love with her. Denham and Jack Driscoll – the ship's first mate, and Ann's love interest – rescue Ann. They head back to New York with Kong in tow, determined to take back the beauty and live in peace with her forever. Ann is recaptured by Kong and finds herself caught between the man she loves and the creature she has come to care deeply for.

The special effects used in *King Kong* were created by Willis O'Brien and the team that worked with him on *The Lost World* (1925). It was Marcel Delgado who, on the instruction of Cooper and O'Brien, constructed the very first Kong model, which was made at a scale meant to represent an 18ft high gorilla. The monster's stature was made to differ from that of a real gorilla because the makers thought it would look more fearsome if Kong was more of an ape-man, and stood straighter.

On Thursday 3 March, 1933, *King Kong* premiered in New York. The film had its world premier at Grauman's Chinese Theatre in Hollywood on 23 March. It opened to rave reviews, packed out cinemas, and made the studio a profit for the first time ever. Interestingly the film was banned in Nazi Germany because censors thought it suggested a threat to Aryan womanhood. Another critic of the film was Fay Wray herself, who regarded her on-screen screaming as 'distracting and excessive'.

King Kong (1933). During the movie, Kong changes size from 18 feet to 24 feet. This was a conscious decision of director Merian C. Cooper who felt that Kong's size wasn't impressive enough in New York. The publicity materials would later state Kong's height was 60 feet, almost 3 times his height in the film.

SON OF KONG
— 1933 —

This sequel to King Kong was released a mere nine months after the original, and starred Robert Armstrong in his second appearance as the film director and showman Carl Denham, who has been hit with several lawsuits following the damage done to New York City by Kong.

Desperate to make some money, Denham leaves New York with the captain of the Venture, Captain Englehorn (played by Frank Reicher), to ship cargo around the Orient. Whilst there, they run into Nils Helstrom, the Norwegian skipper (played by John Marston) who first sold Denham the map to Skull Island. Helstrom informs Denham that there is treasure buried on the island — Helstrom is lying, he just needs someone to help transport him away from the local police — but Denham and Englehorn fall for his story, and set out for Skull Island to find the treasure. Onboard ship they discover a beautiful female stowaway by the name of Hilda (played by Helen Mack), who has escaped from the travelling show run by her recently deceased father (who's death turns out to be the reason Helstrom is on the run). When they land on Skull Island, they meet Kiko, the albino son of Kong. Kiko is nothing like his father; for a start, he's half the size of Kong. His snout is more rounded and his chest is covered in fur. He's also much friendlier, which is fortunate, because ultimately it falls upon Kiko to save the lives of Denham and his team when a deadly earthquake destroys the island.

. . . .

COMEDIC KONG

Ruth Rose, who wrote the script for *Son of Kong*, wisely decided that there was little point in trying to build on the drama and romance of the first film, so she made the sequel funnier and more light-hearted. As a result, Kiko's behaviour is more childlike than Kong's. He's clumsy, and does things without thinking — including knocking over a coconut tree, falling into quicksand and accidentally triggering a shotgun.

. . . .

KONG IN NEW YORK
— 1976 —

The 1976 remake of King Kong was directed by John Guillermin and starred Jeff Bridges, Charles Grodin and Jessica Lange in her first ever movie role. The plot differs quite significantly from the original film, particularly the section leading up to Kong's entrance.

In this film, which is set in the 1970s, Charles Grodin plays Fred Wilson, an executive at Petrox Oil Company, who discovers the existence of an island in the Indian Ocean, which, he believes, may have a huge reserve of oil. Wilson hastily organizes an expedition and sets sail for the mysterious island, but not before a primate palaeontologist named Jack Prescott (played by Jeff Bridges) sneaks on board the ship to warn the crew against stepping foot on the island, for fear of a great beast that is believed to live there. Prescott's warnings fall upon deaf ears, Wilson declares him to be a spy from a rival corporation and has him locked up for the duration of the trip. Later on the journey Wilson's ship chances upon a life raft containing an unconscious actress named Dwan (played by Jessica Lange). She was onboard a director's yacht when it spontaneously exploded. During the course of their journey Jack and Dwan become attracted to one another.

. . . .

THE GOD KONG

When the team finally arrive at their destination they discover that Wilson was right; there is a huge deposit of oil, but it is of such low quality that it is of no commercial value. They meet a tribe of primitive natives who live within the confines of a great wall built to protect them from a mysterious god named Kong. The natives kidnap Dwan, drug her and prepare to offer her to him as a sacrifice. From here on the film follows a similar route to the original. Kong falls in love with Dwan. Prescott and the first mate (played by Ed Lauter) launch a rescue mission which ends with Kong chasing the whole party back to New York City. Instead of clambering up the Empire State Building, this film sees Kong climb up the south tower of the World Trade Centre. The change of venue is no doubt meant to reinforce a major theme of the movie — reckless stupidity caused by capitalist greed.

JACKSON'S GORILLA
— 2005 —

Peter Jackson's 2005 remake of this classic movie stars Naomi Watts as Ann Darrow, Jack Black as Carl Denham and Adrien Brody as Jack Driscoll — who, in this incarnation, is a well-respected scriptwriter instead of the ship's first mate. It is set in the same era as the original film, and follows much the same storyline, with a few key differences. To begin with, it is over an hour longer than its predecessor. It was also much more expensive to make, eventually coming in at a record-breaking $207 million. Kong himself is much bigger and more ape-like than Willis O'Brien's visualization, Jackson having decided in the early stages of production that he did not want Kong to behave like a human. The film's production team studied hours of gorilla footage, and Andy Serkis, the actor who provided the movements for Kong, even went to Rwanda to observe mountain gorillas in the wild.

PETER JACKSON'S DREAM

It is well documented that Jackson had been a huge fan of the original film since childhood. As a 12-year-old, he had attempted to recreate it using his parent's super-8 camera and a model of the monster made of wire, rubber and bits of his mother's fur coat. In 1996, Jackson began working on a 'tongue-in-cheek' treatment for a full-scale remake of *King Kong*. He initially set out to create a comedic film inspired by elements of the *Indiana Jones* franchise, but Universal pulled the plug on the project during the pre-production stages. It wasn't until Jackson achieved massive mainstream success with *The Lord of the Rings* (2001-2003) trilogy, that he finally managed to secure the go ahead for his dream project. By this time, Jackson had abandoned his earlier idea and decided to follow the original plot much more closely. It was a decision he would not live to regret. Despite its length, the film was well received by movie-going audiences and critics alike. Its opening numbers weren't great, but it went on to make $550 million worldwide.

Godzilla
— 1954 —

In the years following his 1954 cinematic debut, *Godzilla* has become one of the most instantly recognizable Japanese film exports of all time. Much like King Kong, this dinosaur-like beast has achieved cult status, and his image now graces everything from album covers and pop videos to t-shirts. Most people are at least vaguely familiar with the plot of the original movie, even if they have never actually seen it:

A Japanese fishing boat is attacked by a flash of light near Odo Island and another ship is sent to investigate, only to meet the same strange fate. The island's older inhabitants believe that a mysterious sea god named 'Godzilla' is responsible for both incidents. Eventually this rumour reaches the mainland, and a helicopter-load of sceptical but interested reporters arrive to document the scene. The islanders perform a nocturnal ceremony to try and keep the beast at bay, but it is to no avail. That night an enormous storm arrives and so does the monster, bringing with it death and destruction to everything that crosses its path. The next day witnesses to the attack begin to arrive in Tokyo, and an archaeologist named Kyohei Yamane decides to take a team to the island whereupon he comes across

a set of enormous radioactive footprints. He concludes that Godzilla must be some kind of prehistoric creature set free by a nuclear explosion, but before Yamane can track down and imprison Godzilla he attacks Tokyo, causing all-out havoc.

....

A NUCLEAR REALITY

This first Godzilla movie struck a particular chord because it was made at a time when the nuclear threat felt very real indeed. Japan was still reeling from America's attack on Hiroshima and Nagasaki, and H bombs were being tested in the Pacific Ocean. In the minds of moviegoers Godzilla became the embodiment of this threat — a malevolent beast unleashed on the innocent people of

A poster for *Godzilla* (1954). Directed by Japanese film-maker Ishiro Honda, the unstoppable dinosaur was originally called Gojira.

Japan because of mankind's unwillingness to leave nature alone.

There are a total of 28 films in the Japanese *Godzilla* franchise and in 1998, Tri Star Pictures released a big budget American remake co-written and directed by Roland Emmerich, director of *Independence Day* (1996) and *2012* (2009). The film was widely panned for leaving out key elements of the story held dear by fans of the Japanese films. A sequel was planned, but shelved because of these negative reviews.

Jurassic Park

— 1993 —

Jurassic Park began life as a novel of the same name by Michael Crichton. It is widely regarded as a cautionary tale, and shares the same sentiment as Mary Shelley's *Frankenstein* and *Godzilla*, in that it warns against the dangers of dabbling in science we can't fully understand or control.

Although a number of the characters differ in terms of age, appearance and their role in driving the story forward, the movie follows the basic plot of the novel:

The eccentric billionaire and InGen CEO, John Hammond (played by Richard Attenborough) has created a 'biological preserve'; a theme park populated by dinosaurs that have been recreated using DNA extracted from prehistoric mosquitoes trapped in amber. When a park worker is attacked by one of the creatures, Hammond's investors insist that a panel of experts are invited to inspect the park and assess its safety. The investors' lawyer Donald Gennaro (played by Martin Ferrero) invites Dr Ian Malcolm (played by Jeff Goldblum), and Hammond invites the palaeontologist Dr Alan Grant (played by Sam Neill), the palaeobotanist Dr

Ellie Sattler (played by Laura Dern), along with his two grandchildren Tim (played by Joseph Mazzello) and Lex (played by Ariana Richards).

Unfortunately for them, Hammond is unaware that his head computer programmer, Dennis Nedry (played by Wayne Knight) is secretly in the employ of one InGen's major corporate rivals. He has been paid to steal fertilized dinosaur embryos from the park, and it is in the course of this theft that he deactivates the park's security system, setting the dinosaurs free and putting everyone in mortal danger.

. . . .

A MOVIE IN THE MAKING

Crichton's novel came to the attention of the major Hollywood studios even before it was published. Crichton had already set his fee at $1.5 million, plus a substantial percentage of the gross, and a number of studios entered into a bidding war, with Universal eventually coming out on top. Steven Spielberg was set to direct and he brought in a team that included Stan Winston, Phil Tippett, Michael Lantieri and Dennis Muren to create the dinosaurs using traditional stop-frame techniques. Animators Mark Dippe and Steve Williams at Industrial Light and Magic created a computer generated walk cycle for the T. Rex skeleton, which changed the direction of the movie's special effects, and the face of animation in general. Palaeontologist Jack Horner was brought in to oversee the design and creation of the creatures because Spielberg felt very strongly that the dinosaurs should be portrayed as animals rather than monsters. It was a wise move. Horner was able to tell the team exactly what the creatures would, and would not have been capable of, and the film is much more credible for it.

Cat People

— 1942 —

....

Cat People is a classic horror movie about a woman who turns into a vicious panther whenever she becomes passionately aroused. It stars Simone Simon as Irena Dubrovna Reed, the Serbian-born fashion designer (and part time panther), and Kent Smith as Oliver Reed, the unfortunate man who marries her.

Irena is deeply in love with her new husband, but dares not sleep with him for fear of transforming into her feline alter ego and ripping him to shreds. Oliver thinks she is delusional and sends her to see a psychiatrist named Dr Judd (played by Tom Conway). Dr Judd diagnoses Irena with a fear of sexual intimacy, but when she discovers that her husband has been spending time alone with his attractive assistant (Alice Moore, played by Jane Randolph) the beast within her is awakened. Strange things start to happen, and it begins to dawn on Alice that she is being stalked by a ferocious creature of the night.

....

MOVIES TO ORDER

Cat People was the first movie made by Val Lewton, a journalist, novelist and poet who was engaged by RKO to make horror movies on a budget of under $150,000 to titles provided by them. Considering its meagre budget, *Cat People* achieved considerable success. It went on to make $4 million — and saved the studio from financial ruin. Following the success of *Cat People* Lewton's bosses decided to give him far more creative freedom. He went on to make a number of other highly successful 'creepy cheapies', including; *I Walked With A Zombie* (1943), *The Leopard Man* (1943), *Isle of the Dead* (1945), and *The Body Snatcher* (1945).

The Exorcist

— 1973 —

....

As demonic movies go, *The Exorcist* is probably the most well-known. It is based on William Peter Blatty's novel of the same name, which is itself based on a 1949 case of demonic possession reputed to have occurred in Cottage City, Maryland, USA involving a young boy named Ronald Hunkeler.

The film tells the story of Regan (played by Linda Blair), an ordinary innocent 12-year-old girl who lives with her actress mother, Chris MacNeil (played by Ellen Burstyn) in Georgetown, Washington DC. Chris begins to notice that Regan is displaying some strange behaviour. At first she attributes this to puberty. Doctors believe there is a lesion on her temporal lobe, but medical tests prove otherwise. Chris takes Regan to see a psychiatrist, but Regan assaults him during her consultation and subsequently her condition worsens, as do the supernatural occurrences surrounding her. In desperation, Chris who is an atheist consults Father Karras (played by Jason Miller) a troubled Jesuit priest who also happens to be a psychiatrist. Father Karras is battling with his own psychological demons following the death of his beloved mother, but he agrees to counsel Regan regardless. To begin with he thinks Regan is suffering from a form of psychosis, but it soon becomes apparent that her case is much more unusual, and sinister than that. A demon has taken hold of Regan's body and soul — and Karras has a fight on his hands if he wants to get her back.

· · · ·

THE FIRST EXORCISM

Father Karras goes to the Church to request permission to perform an exorcism, but his superiors think him too young and inexperienced to take on such a task. They call in Father Lankester Merrin (played by Max von Sydow) an older Jesuit priest who has already battled and exorcized demons, to take over. Karras is chosen to assist him.

The demon antagonist in the film is Pazuzu, a genuine character from Assyrian and Babylonion mythology, who was considered to be the king of the demons of the wind, the son of the god Hanbi. He was believed to be the bearer of storms, and drought, bringing famine during the dry season and locusts during rainy periods. Pazuzu is usually depicted as having the body of a man, the head of a lion, eagle's talons, two pairs of wings and a serpentine penis. Interestingly, although Pazuzu is an evil demon, he is able to give protection from the evil powers of his wife, Lamashtu who causes harm to mothers and their children. He is also able to drive away other evil spirits. Pazuzu is not only named as the demon in the first Exorcist movie, he also features in the first sequel *Exorcist II: The Heretic* (1977).

Linda Blair plays the child possessed by a mysterious demonic entity in *The Exorcist* (1973), directed by William Friedkin.

Curse of the Demon
— 1957 —

Night of the Demon is the British film adaptation of a short story by M. R. James entitled *Casting the Runes*, in which an American psychologist investigates a satanic cult who are suspected of serial murder. In the US the film was made shorter, retitled *Curse of the Demon* and shown as the second half of a double bill alongside *The Revenge of Frankenstein*. Like many supernatural horror movies, the production process was made turbulent because of clashing ideas between cast and crew. Originally they had not planned to show a literal demon (presumably in the belief that the suggestion was scarier than the actuality), but the film's producer Hal E. Chester, inserted one, despite the objections of the writer, director and the film's star, Dana Andrews.

DANA ANDREWS

CURSE
OF THE
DEMON

co starin

PEG

The Omen
— 1976 —

The Omen is generally considered one of the best horror films ever made. It can be instantly recognized by its theme song, *Ave Satani*, which was composed by Jerry Goldsmith. It's a truly creepy song, which really helps to set the tone for a truly creepy movie.

On the surface Katherine and Robert Thorn (played by Lee Remick and Gregory Peck) appear to have everything; they are successful, connected and wealthy, but they desperately want a child. Katherine becomes pregnant, but the baby is stillborn. A priest convinces the grief-stricken Robert to substitute the dead child with an orphan boy, whose mother died at precisely the same moment as their baby. Bizarrely, Robert agrees to take the child, and decides to keep the terrible secret from Katherine. They name the child Damien (interestingly, Damien is also the first name of Father Karras in *The Exorcist*.)

A STRANGE CHILD

Damien is a strange child, to say the least, and strange events seem to occur around him. When his nanny hangs herself at his fifth birthday party, another nanny, Mrs Baylock (Billie Whitelaw) spontaneously arrives accompanied by a large dog. We later discover that Mrs Baylock is a demon sent from Hell to help guard Damien, whose true identity is that of the Antichrist himself. When Katherine falls pregnant with the couple's second child, it sets in motion a series of bizarre and bloody events, as Robert discovers more about his son's true identity and struggles to decide what to do about it.

If a film's success can be judged by the number of times it is satirized and parodied, then *The Omen* surely ranks amongst the most successful films of all time. It was made on a strict budget of $2.8 million, and took $60 million at the box office in the United States alone. It received numerous accolades and spawned two sequels, neither of which exude the same class as the original.

Jeepers Creepers
— 2001 —

This film takes its title from the 1938 song of the same name, which features heavily in the plot. It was written and directed by Victor Salva, who grew up watching 'creature features' and once described himself as a '*Jaws* baby'.

The demon antagonist of the film is 'The Creeper', an ancient and malevolent being who rises every 23rd spring for 23 days to feast on human body parts. Upon consumption these parts are assimilated into its own body. 'It eats lungs so it can breathe, it eats eyes so it can see. Whatever it eats becomes part of it.' This can also be used as a regenerative tool, so if any part of it is injured it can simply hunt down another victim and devour a replacement part. The Creeper seeks out its victims by sensing their fear — unfortunately for siblings Trish and Darry (played by Gina Philips and Justin Long), it has smelled their fear, and found something it particularly likes.

Jeepers Creepers was greeted with mixed reviews. The most common criticism being that, once The Creeper actually appears on screen in all its glory, the fear factor is diminished. Financially though, the film did extremely well, grossing almost $60 million worldwide. A sequel, the predictably entitled *Jeepers Creepers II*, was released in 2003 and made even more money than the original, implying that, in general, audiences enjoyed the first film. A third Jeepers Creepers movie, *Jeepers Creepers 3: Cathedral* is set for release in 2013.

SEA MONSTERS

Creature from the Black Lagoon
— 1954 —

A classic of the B-movie genre, *Creature from the Black Lagoon* was made by Universal Studios, the company that was also responsible for such cult horror movies as *Dracula*, *Frankenstein*, *The Wolf Man* and *The Mummy*. By 1954, audiences no longer considered these supernatural villains scary enough. The nuclear age had descended, and the movie-going public required a new kind of monster. Enter: The Gill-man, the last surviving member of a race of amphibious humanoids.

The Gill-man is a fully amphibious creature, capable of breathing in and out of water. He has superhuman strength and regenerative powers. His scaly skin is so tough that it can withstand a bullet, he can even survive being set on fire. He possesses a dormant set of lungs, which can be used if his gills are damaged. Throughout all three movies in the series it remains unclear whether or not he can be killed, although, presumably, the rest of his race must have died out somehow.

The plot of the film resembles that of *King Kong*, in that it centres around the story of a genetically unique creature who falls in love with, and attempts to abduct, a human woman (Kay Lawrence, played by Julia Adams). In this case though, there is no love lost on the part of the female. Unlike Kong, the Gill-man has no redeeming features, and does not inspire sympathy.

In the original film two men played the

CENTURIES OF PASSION
PENT UP IN HIS SAVAGE HEART!

CREATURE FROM THE BLACK LAGOON

AMAZING! STARTLING! SHOCKING!

...A ADAMS

HARRY ESSEX and ARTHUR ROSS ... WILLIAM ALLAND ...

Creature from the Black Lagoon (1954). The creature is easily one of Universal Studios' most memorable creations. Legend has it, that although Milicent Patrick created the design of the creature, head of Universal Pictures make-up department, Bud Westmore, liked to take full credit for the creature's design.

Gill-man. Actor, diver and underwater cinematographer, Ricou Browning played the monster in the underwater scenes. He would also assume this role in both the film's sequels. On land, Ben Chapman filled his flippers. The creature was based on designs by Disney animator Millicent Patrick and make-up artist Bud Westmore. The suit was created by Jack Kevan, who also worked on *The Wizard of Oz*. It cost $15,000 to make and was extremely uncomfortable to wear. Ben Chapman was unable to sit down for the duration of the time that he wore the suit (about 14 hours a day during filming). It overheated easily, so he chose to spend the majority of his time in a lake on the back-lot.

It Came from Beneath the Sea

— 1955 —

It Came From Beneath The Sea was directed by Robert Gordon and starred Faith Domergue, Donald Curtis and Kenneth Tobey, who also played a leading role in 1953's *The Beast from 20,000 Fathoms*. The script for this movie was designed specifically to make the most of Ray Harryhausen's stop motion animation skills. Like a whole host of B-movies from this era, it explores the fears that arose when Hydrogen bombs began being tested in the world's oceans. Like *Godzilla* and *The Beast from 20,000 Fathoms*, the titular creature is an enormous sea monster (in this case a massive octopus with six arms), that has been forced out of its natural habitat and rendered radioactive thanks to the folly of humankind. Its new-found radioactivity is driving away its food source, so it has taken to attacking whatever it can lay its tentacles on, including passing sea traffic. *It Came from Beneath the Sea* was made on a budget of $150,000. At 79 minutes

long, it is relatively short, but was often paired with Columbia's *Creature with the Atom Brain*, as part of a double bill.

The Call of Cthulhu

— 2005 —

Based on an original short story by H.P. Lovecraft, *The Call of Cthulhu* is a rare beast indeed: a silent movie made at the beginning of the 21st century to mirror the style of 1920s cinema. It was made as an homage to the author, distributed by the H.P. Lovecraft Historical Society and directed by Andrew Leman, who decided to make a black and white silent film in order to show what it would have looked like if it had been made in 1926, when the story was first published.

To achieve their desired effect, Leman and his team used a technique they named Mythoscope — combining modern technology and vintage filming techniques to get the best of both worlds. The result is a film that recreates the Expressionist style of F. W. Murnau, who directed *Nosferatu* amongst many others.

The Call of Cthulhu had previously been thought 'unfilmable' by many Lovecraft fans, so sprawling and complex is the story. Cthulhu is a malevolent entity, something like an octopus or a dragon — 'a pulpy, tentacled head surmounted on a grotesque scaly body with rudimentary wings'. Cthulhu is imprisoned in R'lyeh, an underwater city in the South Pacific, but it is supposed to haunt all of humankind on a subconscious level, as humanity's most basic nightmare. It is worshipped as a god by a number of secretive evil cults. A legend says that one day in the future, he and the rest of the Great Old Ones (over which he is the High Priest) will cease dreaming and return to the earth's surface, causing widespread insanity and mindless violence before destroying mankind for good.

Cloverfield

— 2008 —

....

The unnamed sea monster in *Cloverfield* came into being when producer J. J. Abrams was in Japan promoting *Mission Impossible III*. He came across some Godzilla toys while he was in a toyshop with his son and it occurred to him that America needed its own Godzilla-style monster — something with more bite than *King Kong*, who he considered a little too charming for contemporary audiences.

The Cloverfield monster is portrayed as an immature creature who is suffering from 'separation anxiety', in much the same way that a young elephant might lash out when taken away from its mother. The director, Matt Reeves, created this back-story out of a belief that 'there's nothing scarier than something huge, that's spooked.' The artist

and concept designer Neville Page created the designs for the monster, and came up with a biological rationale for why the creature looks the way it does. The preparatory sketches on his website show something that, to begin with, looks like a dragon/human/alien hybrid, with overlong arms that resemble an ape's and the head of a fish.

Inspiration for the film came from *Godzilla* and *King Kong*, and also from *Them!* and *The Beast From 20,000 Fathoms*, but unlike *Godzilla* or the American B movies of the 1950s, the *Cloverfield* monster has nothing to do with atomic energy. It is not radioactive, and it is not awoken from its lair as a result of nuclear weapons testing. The way the film is presented — as found footage from a handheld video camera discovered by the United States Department of Defence in the area of New York City 'formerly known as Central Park', suggests that maybe the collective 'fear du jour' has shifted away from nuclear war to something more unpredictable and insidious: the clear and present threat of global terrorism.

Cloverfield (2008). Shot as if from a handheld camcorder, the sub-plot is established by showing pieces of video previously recorded on the tape that are being recorded over. However, to be honest, it is doubtful that any store-bought camcorder would survive the traumatic events of this movie!

The Beast From 20,000 Fathoms
— 1953 —

The Beast From 20,000 Fathoms is a science fiction film about a gargantuan prehistoric creature that is awoken from its 100 million year hibernation by a nuclear bomb test in the Arctic Circle. It was Eugene Lourie's directorial debut, and one of three 'dinosaur' movies he made in a career that spanned over three decades. The movie's titular monster is described as a Rhedosaurus. It looks like a dinosaur, but in fact it displays several features that no dinosaur possessed. He has semi-sprawling limbs and his skull is unlike that of a prehistoric creature. It is thought that the 'Rh' in the Rhedosaurus's name is a nod to Ray Harryhausen, who designed the creature effects for the film.

WARNER BROS. PRESENT

"The Beast From 2

! A THRILL STORY BEYOND ALL IMAGINING!

0,000 Fathoms"

53 \ 358

INDEX

Picture Credits

This edition published in 2012 by
CHARTWELL BOOKS, INC.
A division of BOOK SALES, INC.
276 Fifth Avenue Suite 206
New York, New York 10001
USA

© 2012 Omnipress Limited
Canary Press
An imprint of Omnipress Ltd
The Business Suite
Enterprise Centre
Eastbourne
East Sussex BN21 1BD
England
www.omnipress.co.uk

Although every effort has been made to trace and contact people mentioned in the text for their approval in time for publication, this has not been possible in all cases. If notified, we will be pleased to rectify any alleged errors or omissions when we reprint the title.

ISBN-13: 978-0-7858-2880-8
ISBN-10: 0-7858-2880-X

Printed in China